THE NECESSITY OF COMMUNISM

by

JOHN MIDDLETON MURRY

LONDON
JONATHAN CAPE
TORONTO

FIRST PUBLISHED 1932

JONATHAN CAPE LTD.   30 BEDFORD SQUARE   LONDON
AND 91 WELLINGTON STREET WEST, TORONTO
JONATHAN CAPE & HARRISON SMITH INC.
139 EAST 46TH STREET NEW YORK

The bracketed figures refer to
notes at the end of book
(page 127 *et seq.*)

PRINTED IN GREAT BRITAIN IN THE CITY OF OXFORD
AT THE ALDEN PRESS
PAPER BY JOHN DICKINSON & CO., LTD.
BOUND BY A. W. BAIN & CO., LTD.

CONTENTS

'Finally, when the class war is about to be fought to a finish, disintegration of the ruling class and the old order of society becomes so active, so acute, that a small portion of the ruling class breaks away to make common cause with the revolutionary class, the class which holds the future in its hands. Just as in former days part of the nobility went over to the bourgeoisie, so now part of the bourgeoisie goes over to the proletariat. *Especially does this happen in the case of some of the bourgeois ideologues, who have achieved a theoretical understanding of the historical movement as a whole.*'

The Manifesto of the Communist Party. By Karl Marx and Friedrich Engels.

FOREWORD

COMMUNISM? What do you mean by Communism?

The whole of this book is an answer to that question: Therefore I beg of my readers not to approach it with any pre-formed idea of what Communism is: for it is certain at this moment that this pre-formed idea will be derived from Russian Communism. And one vital thesis of this book is that such an alien derivation of the idea of Communism is fatal, to Communists, to this nation, and to the world.

It is fatal because in England Communism *must* be English. If Communism does not feel and obey the inward necessity of becoming English, then Communism will never gain a hold of this country.

'How admirable!' you may say. 'We desire nothing better than to keep the vile thing out.'

But wait! A still more vital thesis of this book is that Communism will *inevitably* come to this country. You cannot stop it. No power on earth can stop it.

'But you speak paradoxes! You say: in certain circumstances Communism will never gain a hold of this country – and you say Communism is inevitable. How can you expect a sane man to listen to you?'

Well, think a moment! Those propositions are, verbally, in contradiction. But obviously, if Communism does not mean the same thing in each of them, they may both be true. In fact, they both *are* true.

And the whole point is that Communism is not *one* thing. This book will show you how and why.

Now, there are two main classes of people in this country to whom Communism is one thing: the first, those who see red, the second, those who wave red, at the word. And the moment we have so described them, we realize that the *one* thing that Communism is to them, is Russian Communism.

I do not believe that this book will make much impression on either of these, though candidly, I have far more hope of reaching the 'reds' than the 'whites.' But the book is not primarily addressed to them. It is addressed to people who are neither the one nor the other. It is addressed to them for two reasons: first, because they are neither the one nor the other; and, second, because they are decisive for the future of this country, and ultimately – as I believe and will try to show – for the future of the world.

For these people, I believe, are capable of seeing two things: one, that Communism in some form *is* inevitable in this country; two, that Russian Communism is impossible in this country. The man who is or may be capable of seeing both these things is the man to whom this book is addressed.

Such a man will see the second proposition: that Russian Communism is impossible in this country, far more easily than he will see the first: that Communism in some form is inevitable in this country. In another book, perhaps, I shall be able to show him how, deep in his unconsciousness, the second of these propositions is immediately involved in the first: that, ultimately, it is because we Englishmen know that Russian Communism is impossible in this country, that (although we do not know this yet) some deliberate form of Communism is inevitable in this country.

The simple form taken by this instinctive feeling of the impossibility of Russian Communism in England is that the Englishman is too 'decent' to allow such inhuman horrors to be perpetrated. For the horrors of Russian Communism have been, and still are, inhuman. Let no irresponsible sentimental sympathiser with the U.S.S.R. delude himself about conditions there. Here is the end of a report, published on the day I write, of a conference of prison authorities for Russia proper.

At a recent conference at the State Institute on the study of crime Krylenko, the Commissar of Justice, explained that the Soviet Government was now working out a new theory for prison work 'which repudiates as a political error attempts to reform class enemies.' Such prisoners must be used for Socialist purposes, but warders must abandon the practice of regarding them as individuals. They must be regarded collectively as an alien mass.

Utevsky, the penitentiary specialist, told the conference that it was necessary to offer 'class enemies' certain privileges only as a means of getting better results from their labour. All attempts to reform them must be avoided. They must be isolated, subdued, and trained for manual gang labour. Professional criminals must be subjected to different treatment. Criminals left from the Tsarist regime were naturally dying out, but under the Soviet regime it was estimated that about 10,000 new professional criminals had appeared. These should receive the advantage of reforming influences and be reclaimed as far as possible for factory life.

The Times, November 13, 1931.

That is not anti-Soviet propaganda. It is the pure logic of Russian Communism. Consider its implications. The professional 'murderer with violence' will be reformed; the man who happens to hold heretical views concerning the Russo-Marxian dogma is deliberately to be treated as a mere beast of burden, worked to death, and exterminated.

It is, I believe, unimaginable in this country; and because it is unimaginable, it is not real to us. Nevertheless, it is happening. And it is because we have a dim sense of these inhuman horrors, that we feel in our hearts that Russian Communism is impossible in this country.

But why do we feel that? It is simply our instinctive humanity that makes us feel that such deliberate inhumanity is for ever impossible in England. But now, look closer! Humanity is not a thing you can depend on in the modern world. At the very moment when we have reached the point at which we revolt individually against such inhumanity, the world has become such that our individual feelings of humanity are impotent.

In the complex modern world of competitive capitalism the vast majority of our individual actions are de-individualized. I may, personally, be as humane as I like, but unless I am a man of uncommon imagination, I shall not be aware that I am involved in a system which is radically inhuman: that just as the system

of Russian Communism necessitates this ghastly inhumanity to men like you and me, so does the system of
economic individualism necessitate ghastly inhumanity
to men of another class. The Russian Communist has
one unanswerable reply to those who would point
him to the horrors of his system. He points us to the
horrors of ours. We say: 'But ours are necessary;
they are due to the working of the iron laws of economics.' He replies: 'But ours are necessary, too; ours
are due to the working of the iron laws of Communism.'
And he goes one better: he says 'We are at least conscious of our inhumanity, you are unconscious of yours.
Ours is deliberate, willed to an end – the regeneration
of the world. Yours just happens, and is unwilled –
also to an end – the degeneration of the world.'
There is no answer. The Russian Communist has won.

And why has he won? Not, believe me, because of
any dialectical subtlety, but because in the last resort
in the strange world in which we live, individual
decency *is* impotent. To be revolted, individually, by
the inhumanity of Russian Communism is no guarantee
against its happening, here and to us. To withstand its
menace, there is one way alone: that our individual
humanity should become corporate. We must awake
to the simple fact that in the modern world of economic
individualism, de-individualized by the capitalist
system, it is impossible for the individual to be humane.
He may think he is humane, as we all do, but it is
impossible for him to *be* humane. Hence the feeling of
impotence among so many individually humane men
to-day.

For to-day individualism is finally divided against
itself. It is in its death agony. We have fought through

centuries for the freedom of the individual: we seemed on the way to achieve it: it is our native sense of the freedom of the individual that is revolted by Russian inhumanity – 'Warders must abandon the practice of regarding them as individuals.' And yet we ourselves are not free enough to be able to *be* humane. It is fantastic, it is paradoxical, but it is true.

And there lies the choice before conscious men at this crucial moment of our history. Is our individual humanity to become conscious, to become real, to become effective? If so, we must give up, deliberately and consciously, our economic individualism. That may, in those abstract terms, sound easy. It is not easy. If this book does nothing else, it many convince you of the sternness of the sacrifice that is required from you.

The only guarantee you have against the horrors of Russian Communism is that your feelings of humanity should be real. Not sincere feelings. Sincere feelings are not real in the world to-day. But active, completely effective feelings. Unless your humanity becomes completely effective, completely corporate, you will get the inhumanity of Russian Communism, *and you will have deserved to get it.*

In other words the only remedy against Russian Communism in this country is English Communism. That is why Communism is invincible in the modern world. It can be defeated only by itself in a finer form. If you do not want inhuman Communism, then you must have human Communism. If you do not want a revolution in the world about you, you must undergo a revolution within. This book is, incidentally, the record of that inward revolution in a single man.

If it sets it in motion in you also, then have no fear. The cause of human Communism will be won.

Finally, it should be said that this book aims merely at giving a rough and hasty outline of a *completer* conception of Marxian Communism than any that obtains in this country, or in Russia. Nevertheless, I have had to refrain from any attempt to do real justice to Marx as a philosopher and as a 'religious' thinker. As far as I can see, Marxists, both English and Russian, are absurdly ignorant of Marx's eminence in both these capacities. I do not think it would be exaggeration to say that Marx's *Thesen über Feuerbach* – a bare five hundred words of compressed and pregnant thinking – are completely unknown to the average English Marxist.

The fact is that Marxism has suffered a deplorable degradation both in England and in Russia. In England it has been quietly emasculated; in Russia noisily coarsened. The author of the *Thesen über Feuerbach* would have been astonished at the crudity of Lenin's *Materialism and Empirio-Criticism*. Marx's materialism is comprehensive and pregnant in the highest degree; Lenin's oppressive and stifling. That is not to say, Leninism is *not* Marxism; but it is only one very particular, national manifestation of Marxism, valid for Russia, ridiculous in England. 'Communism' in this country has become imitation Leninism, and is perfectly futile. I will give, by way of simple illustration, two passages from Marx and Engels respectively, which the professional 'Communist' would do well, first to understand and then to meditate.

'Social life is essentially practical. All the mysteries,

which divert pure theory into Mysticism, find their rational resolution in human activity, and in the understanding of this activity.' (Marx: *Über Feuerbach VIII.*)

'We must retort to Stirner that the human heart is by nature and immediately, in its egoism, disinterested and self-sacrificing, and that thus he is forced back again into the thing (Altruism) that he fights . . . But if the total organism (*leibhaftige Individuum*) is accepted as the true basis, the true starting-point of our "Man," it goes without saying that Egoism – naturally not Stirner's egoism of the intelligence alone, but also the Egoism of the heart – is the starting-point of our love of humanity; otherwise it floats in air.' (Engels to Marx: Nov. 19th, 1844).

When our professional 'Communists' have learned a little of Engels' 'egoism of the heart,' and have a glimpse of the 'mysteries' which Marx, like Goethe before him, acknowledged and more bravely resolved than Goethe, we shall be nearer to an understanding.

16

THE NECESSITY OF COMMUNISM

B

THE TANGLE AND THE CLUE

AN agonizing spiritual issue is being fought to the death, or to the life, in the world to-day; but the true nature of this issue is hard for us to apprehend. This difficulty is inevitable, for on those who are most conscious that a spiritual struggle is being waged the temptation is almost irresistible to formulate it in terms that are already familiar and blunted. But this formulation of the struggle in familiar terms, however great an advance it may be on a mere unconsciousness of its existence, has the dangerous consequence of blinding us to the fact that the world is in travail of something *new*. Because we fail, in our finest consciousness, to be aware of the newness that is imminent in the world at large and may be imminent in ourselves, we grow weary, we grow old. We turn to Faith, because we have no faith.

The modern conflict, as it is familiarly formulated, is the conflict between Religion and Materialism. On the Continent, and in the minds of those thinkers in England who are not insulated from Continental influences, it appears, more definitely, as the conflict between Christianity and Marxism. Once it is allowed to crystallize into those terms, the deadlock is apparent and the weariness of stagnation begins to settle on the minds which so conceive the conflict. Yet a little reflection, or perhaps a good deal of reflection, or perhaps again the obscure instinct that such stagnation and deadlock must be superficial, an antithesis of the consciousness superimposed on the unconscious effort of the life within, leads us to one clear and undubitable perception: that what is dynamic in Christianity, and what is dynamic in Marxism has its origin in a common source.

Unfortunately, Marx is a name. He is more often criticised than read; more often conjured than consulted. But those who have really surrendered themselves to his great work – *Das Kapital* – with minds equally receptive to the actual revolution in our attitude to social and economic issues for which he laboured, and to the mighty groundswell of ethical passion which animated and inspired him in his heroic task, know to what company he belongs. He belongs to the company of the great Hebrew prophets – of whom the most universal was Jesus – the prophets whose souls were kindled by the sight of oppression and injustice, and who in the old times poured their indignation into the mouth of God.

It is the ethical passion of Karl Marx which has made him the mightiest spiritual force in the modern world. Whence, otherwise, comes his power over the hearts and minds of men? It might plausibly be said Marx's historical materialism is a great scientific theory (as it is) and that the men of the nineteenth century were prepared to receive it by the influence of biological materialism; that in his work men accustomed to the biological materialism of Darwin saw, for the first time, the triumphant application of the same principles to the social and economic phenomena of human history. But that, alas, would be plausible only to the ignorant. The men of biological materialism in the animal world had no ear for Marx. Scientific materialism was the preserve of the great industrial middle-classes; they saw to it, instinctively, that it should not spread to provinces where it must conflict with their interests. They could welcome Darwinism. Did it not supply the theology for *Laissez-faire?* 'Each for himself and the Devil take the hindmost' was revealed as the law of Nature, and of God. Darwinism was heaven-sent, but Marxism came from the Devil. For how could it possibly be the will of God that the blessed system of economic individualism should perish by its own inherent viciousness?

No, it was not the spread of scientific materialism into biology that prepared the ground for the acceptance of Marxism. Nor was Marxism accepted. Scientists, in spite of modern cant, are no more disinterested than bishops; they are governed, unconsciously, by the taboos of the classes in which they flourish. The middle-class scientist can no more look at the phenomenon of class scientifically than the capitalist can. For to be truly scientific is to be disinterested. And how shall a man be disinterested where his own interests are directly involved? It is hard indeed.

Marxism was not welcomed by science; it was ignored by science. The ground was prepared for the reception of Marxism, first, by the mere existence of that class whose fundamental identity of interest Marx first made clear – the proletariat – Labour treated as a mere commodity, although Labour *is* labouring men and women; and, second, by the existence of a few individuals of other classes who were, like Marx himself, animated and inspired by the ethical passion of disinterested sympathy with those less fortunate than themselves.

It is doubtless arbitrary to confine ethical passion to the passion of disinterested sympathy with those less fortunate than ourselves. This is rather the distinctively new form slowly taken by ethical passion in the Western world when the influence of Judaism reached it in the universal ethic proclaimed by Christ. There was, of course, ethical passion in Platonism and Stoicism, which has endured; but though it has endured, it is not distinctive. The distinctive ethical passion of the epoch to which we belong is the Judaeo-Christian passion of disinterested sympathy. To this passion, primarily, Marx made his appeal; this passion he conspicuously inherited. Whether or not he consciously acknowledged his derivation from Jesus, it is manifest.

Keats, in a moment of selfless striving after self-knowledge from which he emerged a changed man, declared that in all human history he could catch a glimpse of only two 'completely disinterested' men. They were Socrates and Jesus. True, the history of mankind is not quite so barren as it then appeared to Keats's hungry eyes. He himself was to give the world a beautiful pattern of what disinterestedness might be. But disinterestedness is rare, infinitely rarer than it is pretended to be. Most of those who claim the virtue, most of those who have been accorded it, are mere usurpers.

How should it not be so? Consider simply the enormous paradox by which orthodox Christianity, rooted historically in the life and teaching and death of a completely disinterested man, has made it theoretically impossible for any one who believed in it to be himself disinterested. The expectation of reward, the fear of punishment in the life hereafter, makes nonsense of the very notion of disinterestedness. In a world of beliefs in which that reward, that punishment are real, disinterestedness is strictly inconceivable. Hence the familiar yet still salutary epigram, that there has been only one Christian, and he died on the Cross. The judgment, though salutary, is extreme. There have in fact been many Christians in all times who have risen clean beyond the belief in a life of reward and punishment to come. They have known, by experience, that eternal life does not wait upon mortal death: that it is to be had, for the seeking, now: that it does not belong to the same order as the life which is ended by death. All these things they have known, and in the process of learning them, they have followed the pattern of their master, and lived anew the simple miracle of his life. They, too, have become completely disinterested.

None the less, orthodox Christianity, and there is little Christianity still professing the name which is not orthodox in this cardinal matter of conceiving eternal life as a prolongation of our life in time, makes of disinterestedness a heresy. Therefore we may unfeignedly rejoice that Christianity is steadily losing ground in the modern world. It is true that, in the majority of men, the lapse from Christianity means the falling into creeds, or sheer ignorances, infinitely less valuable than Christianity was when it was real. But the lapse from nominal Christianity will hasten the coming of the crucial and pregnant moment, when Christianity as an institution will be faced with the dilemma: disinterestedness or extinction. For Christianity, as it now exists, these are equivalents. For Christianity to become disinterested is for Christianity to will its own annihilation. But not quite. The heresy of disinterestedness, the heresy of Jesus, will emerge unscathed.

THE PARADOX OF MARXISM

TRUE disinterestedness is rare. For it makes a very great demand on the man who seeks to achieve it. And this demand is two-fold; it is at once an intellectual and a moral demand. Let us begin with the intellectual demand.

Intellectual disinterestedness demands that we should be *complete* materialists. It is difficult to be a complete materialist; it is fatally easy to be an incomplete one. The modern world is encumbered with facile and false and fashionable materialists, of whom the self-styled 'Behaviourists' are chief. They think they have discovered the secret of the universe in Pavlov's experiments upon the conditioned reflexes; whereas those valuable experiments merely indicate that experimental biology may begin to grope towards a truth clearly enunciated by the great Jew, Benedict Spinoza, more than 250 years ago.

The 'behaviour' of the human animal is an infinitely various thing. The shallow materialist thinks he has discovered the secret of human behaviour in a conditioned reflex. His vision is so narrow that he actually cannot see what human behaviour *is*. The plays of Shakespeare are human behaviour; the sayings of Jesus are human behaviour; the writings of Karl Marx are human behaviour. All these wonderful and precious things are, simply and finally, the imperishable record of the gestures of individual animals of a particular species of the genus *homo*. They are, so to speak, frozen animal gestures.

The false and stupid materialist imagines that, because these things are animal gestures, they can be *reduced* to animal gestures of the same order as the flick of a frog's leg. But even to credit him with that is to do him too much honour. He is so hopelessly blinkered that he cannot even see that these precious things *are* animal gestures. In other words, his Behaviourism simply leaves out of the very world he pretends to explain all that momentous and wonderful behaviour with which the human animal is most deeply and intimately concerned. He tells us sagely that the day of introspection is over; only objective realities are real for him. He does not know what he means. Is 'Antony and Cleopatra' not an objective reality? It manifestly is. How does our facile Behaviourist propose to explain that piece of public behaviour? He does not propose to explain it. It has never yet occurred to him that it is, simply, behaviour. He is an ignorant and false materialist.

Man is a wholly conditioned animal; he is a total organism. But in order to know what kind of an organism he is we must scrutinize not the behaviour of dogs in the laboratory, but the total history of mankind in politics, in religion, in art, and supremely in the behaviour of those individual men who have made the deepest impression on the organic substance of the race. Not that the history of the human animal is simply the history of the supreme individual. It is not. It is also, and equally, the history of mankind in the mass. We must scrutinize with serene impartiality both the one and the other, as forming, in their complex combination, the actual recorded behaviour of the human animal.

One would have thought it obvious; but, alas, it has hardly even begun to penetrate the minds of our 'scientific' materialists. They tell one another that human biology is a science, and that the decisive test is experimental. Will they kindly repeat, under experimental conditions, the process that gave rise to the behaviour that is Karl Marx's *Das Kapital*? Are they really such fools as to believe that one day they will be able to arrange conditions in their laboratories so that a human animal exposed to them will exhibit the interesting behaviour of Karl-Marx-writing-Capital?

Once the problem is seen in those simple terms the fallacy of Behaviourism shrieks to heaven. Not merely are the experimental conditions demanded by the most significant kinds of behaviour nothing less than the whole of human life, the whole context of human history, but the human animal itself who is to exhibit this behaviour must be one capable of an altogether exceptional delicacy of organic response – intellectual and moral. That all the experience of which the rarest human being is capable is simply the response of an organism to stimulus is perfectly true; but to suppose that the organic responsiveness or the organic stimulus can be represented quantitatively – to conceive, for instance, that the life-experience which was the material environment of the organism called John Keats is capable of being measured on a *vernier* – is an infantile delusion. The modern mechanistic biologist is completely devoid of imagination.

He prides himself upon it. There is no nonsense about him. Unfortunately, there is no sense about him either; and that simply because he lacks imagination. For true imagination is not fantasy; it is simply the capacity of seeing things precisely as they are. The world of human beings, the history of humanity, is not a world of frogs or the history even of a race of great apes; it is a world of *human* animals, the history of the *human* race – of a race which, rather than accept the doctrines of a stupid and degrading materialism, has persisted in believing, in the face of all evidence, in a supernatural God and a supernatural soul. This belief is now become stupid and degrading also; but it is by no means so utterly stupid and degrading as the shallow materialism which is fashionable to-day.

The world of Existence does not have to be reduced and simplified and denatured to become the world of Matter; it *is*, in all the splendour of its extant variety, the world of Matter.

In other words, the only true materialism is the materialism which has imagination enough to comprehend that it must provide securely within its own material world for what are called 'values.' Such a materialism was first clearly enunciated by Spinoza, from him it reached Goethe and Hegel, who corrupted it; it was rescued from corruption by Feuerbach, and from Feuerbach it passed to Marx. Marxian materialism is in origin Spinozistic; in Marx it found an adequate imagination, and a new language of expression. Darwinism gave Marx an instrument for describing with an accuracy never approached before the historical process of mankind in society. The seemingly unimaginative doctrine of historical materialism was one of the supreme efforts of the human imagination, which shallow minds are incapable of comprehending. Marx neglected, quite deliberately, the actual consideration of the more individual and private values; he could afford to neglect them, for he incorporated them. Truth and imagination were embodied in him. Intellectual disinterestedness went hand in hand with ethical disinterestedness. Karl Marx was not a fashionable professor nor a smug economist; he was a man who devoted his life to a cause, who was hounded from country to country because he dared to speak a gospel which poor men knew in their hearts was true, and rich men feared like death. Marx did not have to worry about 'values,' because he *was* value.

For 'values,' as I have shown elsewhere, are real only in so far as they are embodied in the actual organisms of individual men. The 'values' of Christianity, for example, are real only in the actual behaviour of human beings. If they are not real in human behaviour they are not real at all. And in the behaviour of Karl Marx, suddenly, the values of Christianity were real. Of course, they looked devilishly un-Christian; simply because there is nothing more un-Christian than real Christianity. If you make real in your behaviour 'Blessed are the *poor*,' or the saying: 'It is easier for a camel to go through the eye of a needle than for a rich man to enter the kingdom of God,' you begin to turn the world upside down; and with one voice the bishops and the curates and the congregations committed to their charge will tell you that there is nothing more utterly un-Christian than that.

This is not a matter of religion; it is a matter of *complete* historical materialism. For Marx's historical materialism was not quite complete. To put it quite simply, the only thing that is not explained by Marxism is Marx himself; the only fact about modern society that is not accounted for in *Das Kapital* is the fact that Marx starved himself to write it. If he had been a fashionable professor or a smug economist it would have been explicable that he should have written a fat book; only it would not have been *Das Kapital*. It would have been a smug and fashionable book. But here was a man devoting himself with utter disinterestedness, enduring heart-rending hardship and poverty, in order to write a great work to show how all social relations were based on interestedness.

Here then is the vital paradox. Marxism is true, it is the only living truth to-day. Yet Marxism does not include Marx himself. There is no room in it for the action of an utterly disinterested man. Evidently, Marxism is a queer thing; evidently, it is our business to understand it; evidently, it is our duty to make Marxism complete by making it include Marx himself. We can be content with nothing less.

This then is the task of this little book – to create a Marxism that shall include Marx himself. It was like Marx to leave himself out of his own world. We shall repay his heroism by putting him into it again.

SPIRIT AND MATTER

The basic vision of historical Materialism is not peculiar to Marx. Wherever true spirituality is present, there true materialism is never far away. The great mystics, the great philosophers – for instance, Aristotle and Spinoza – were always potential, and often actual, historical materialists. The vision will be found in the prologue to the third book of Spinoza's *Ethics*; it is distinctly uttered in a wonderful passage of Keats's letters, which needs to be quoted and quoted again until its message sinks into men's hearts and minds.

Very few men have ever arrived at a complete disinterestedness of Mind: very few have been influenced by a pure desire of the benefit of others – in the greater part of the Benefactors of Humanity some meretricious motive has sullied their greatness – some melodramatic scenery has fascinated them. From the manner in which I feel Haslam's misfortune I perceive how far I am from any humble standard of disinterestedness. Yet this feeling ought to be carried to its highest pitch, as there is no fear of its ever injuring society – which it would do, I fear, pushed to an extremity. For in wild nature the Hawk would lose his Breakfast of Robins and the Robin his of Worms – the Lion must starve as well as the Swallow. The greater part of Men make their way with the same instinctiveness, the same unwandering eye from their purposes, the same animal eagerness as the Hawk. The Hawk wants a Mate, so does the Man – look at them both, they set about it and procure one in the same manner – they get their food in the same manner. The noble animal Man for his amusement smokes his pipe – the Hawk balances about the clouds – that is the only difference of their leisures. This it is that makes the Amusement of Life – to a speculative Mind – I go among the Fields and catch a glimpse of a Stoat or a field-mouse peeping out of the withered grass – the creature hath a purpose, and its eyes are bright with it. I go amongst the buildings of a city and see a man hurrying along – to what? the creature has a purpose and his eyes are bright with it. But then, as Wordsworth says, 'we have all one human heart. . . .' There is an electric fire in human nature tending to purify – so that among these human creatures there is continually some new birth of new heroism. The pity is, that we must wonder at it, as we should at finding a pearl in rubbish.

There is Marxism; and there is Marx. To see the world of Existence thus is to see it in its simple truth. The great achievement of Marx was to have pursued the vision home, to have seen the working of animal instinct run wild in the vast and complicated mechanism of modern industry, which multiplied and intensified its effects and did not change its nature.

Only the shallow minds will be surprised at the notion of an essential congruity between the vision of Marx and the vision of great mystics, great poets, and great philosophers. There is, as I have said, a radical affinity between true spirituality and true materialism. Each necessitates the other; each demands a veritable detachment.

Detachment sounds a cold virtue, to those who know nothing of it. By them it is idly supposed to be the same as indifference; and indifference, in common language, means indifference to the fate of others and a complacent concentration on one's own well-being. The indifference of true detachment is precisely the reverse of this. It involves and necessitates indifference towards oneself, and concern with the fate of others. For detachment means the disentangling of the impersonal Self, which is Spirit, from the personal self, which is Matter. By this we raise ourselves, in our impersonality, clean beyond the flux of existence to which our personal selves wholly belong. We pass beyond the world of Good and Evil; but it is not *we* who pass. *We*, the living and personal beings that we are, cannot pass beyond the world of Good and Evil. In it we live, and move, and, so long as we live, we cannot escape it. It is Spirit which alone can escape it and rise free. Spirit, it is true, is indifferent, because, being impersonal, it cannot be otherwise. It looks down on the world of Good and Evil and declares that it is good, but it is good not with the goodness that is opposed to evil, but with the goodness of the meta-physical perfection that must necessarily, and does evidently, inhere in every atom of Existence.

As persons we cannot behold that perfection; as Spirit we can. As Spirit, we can behold our own perfection. But to lay claim to that perfection as persons would be morally monstrous, and intellectually a paralogism. Our personal perfection is something for

c   33

which we have to struggle in the world of good and evil, to which our personalities wholly belong. That is no true spiritual vision which does not ultimately issue in a new potency for good in the world of existence. Our recognition of this truth depends upon the clearness with which we recognize the absolute heterogeneity of Spirit and Matter. The perfection which Spirit discerns in the world of Matter is not a moral perfection; it is a simple and wonderful uniqueness shared alike by the moral monster and the pattern of human virtues. To translate a spiritual and impersonal recognition of the perfection of Existence into a personal assertion that the human world is morally perfect is an offence against both morality and reason. It can only be committed by those who know the world of Spirit at second-hand.

So, people who write about mysticism argue that the mystical vision involves an abstention from good works in the world in Time: since everything, at any moment, is perfect, what motive, they ask, is there for any action rather than any other? As though a creature, because he has passed beyond creatures, must not return to creatures again: he has been refreshed, he has been renewed, he has been reborn, but he remains in Existence. The problems of Existence are there before him, they with their old urgency, he with a new indifference, not to them but to the vicissitudes of his own personal being. For these profound equivocators, who would deduce the moral perfection of the world of our personal experience from the metaphysical perfection of the world of impersonal experience, no punishment could be too heavy. They poison the wells. It was against such as these that Marx's indignation

34

flamed most furiously: for the form that is taken by this equivocation in the order with which he was concerned is the complacent assertion that History is always right: *Die Geschichte hat immer recht.* In fact, history has never been right, and never will be; but there is a possibility that if the energies of chosen human beings are turned towards righting the history which it is in their power to influence, history will come to be more nearly right than it has been before. The only rightness which belongs to all history is the metaphysical rightness, the material necessity, of everything that has been or is; its moral rightnesses have been few and far between. The gulf between the recognition that the process of history has been necessary, and the assertion that we have no power to change it, is the gulf of an absolute heterogeneity: it is impassable.

To look on the world as it is is to know that it could not be otherwise than it is; but that vision and that knowledge are dynamic in their effects. Just as in the individual person the recognition that his personal being belongs wholly to the process of Existence, is an immense liberation of himself, a purification from which he emerges with his creaturely energies renewed; so in the body politic the recognition, which must happen through individual persons who are part of it, that it too is wholly conditioned, is the liberation of a new power to change it. Just as when we learn to objectify our *total* selves, and discover that we are not responsible for our vices or our virtues, for the first time the sense of our true responsibility descends upon us, so when we learn to objectify the historical process, which is as it were our own extended personal past, and absolve this historical person from responsibility for its own configuration, we then for the first time learn the pattern to which all effective effort must conform, and are liberated to the work. In society as in individuals it is knowledge of destiny that makes men free to be themselves. As Engels wrote in *Anti-Dühring*, 'Freedom is knowledge of necessity. Necessity is blind only in so far as it is not understood.'

THE MISSION OF MARX

MARX's function towards society was to bring it to a knowledge of its destiny. He, first among men, achieved a disinterested vision of the cardinal process of modern history. He showed how the capitalist system of his day actually worked, and how if the process were not controlled it must inevitably lead to disaster. This is not the moment to expound his actual doctrine. It must suffice for the present that he found a contradiction inherent in the process of competitive capitalism, which must inevitably bring it to an end. A new kind of social organization must take its place.

What he actually foresaw, generalizing from English conditions in the 'fifties, was a progressive deterioration in the position of the class which has only its labour to sell – the proletariat. Between this class and the other class, which owned or controlled the means of production, he foresaw a constantly increasing conflict of interest, which could only be terminated by the proletariat seizing to themselves those means of production which had been accumulated out of the 'surplus value' created by themselves alone and would be concentrated in the hands of fewer and fewer. This 'expropriation of the expropriators' would be a revolution, and it seemed to him necessarily (except in England) a violent one.[1] Thus his doctrine appeared to assume the simple form of a necessary intensification of class-war, and an inevitable violent revolution.

If the class-war, and the ultimate revolution are inevitable, argue the critics of Marxism, why attempt to hasten it?

> The 'materialist interpretation of history' bears the imprint of its idealistic German origin, it might better be called the *fatalistic*, or even the conventional interpretation of history. I have no quarrel with Marx's 'materialistic interpretation' of past history, which is intelligent and within limits very illuminating, but this materialistic interpretation seems to me simply incompatible with desiring anything. (*T. S. Eliot.*)

Behind such a criticism lies the radical failure to grasp the heterogeneity of Spirit and Matter on which we have insisted. Because I see that my animal body, including my ethical passion, is totally conditioned, wholly belonging to the world of Existence and necessity, I do not cease to feel ethical passion. Because I recognize its origins are not transcendental, that it is not, in the pure sense, spiritual at all, I do not cease to be moved by it. My ethical passion is integral to my organic constitution, as much a part of me as the colour of my eyes. It is wholly 'material,' in the strict sense, and absolutely real.

So in the larger body of the social organism, the recognition that it has obeyed a destiny is not in the least incompatible with the passionate desire and firm conviction that that 'destiny' may be changed by individual action. On the contrary, the recognition of 'destiny' in the past is the condition of making our energies effective in the present and for the future.

For the recognition of 'destiny' in history is the simple seeing of the situation as it was and is. That simple seeing does not deny the existence in the past, still less now, of individuals moved by ethical passion. On the contrary, an essential part of its objective estimation of the situation is a measuring of the weight and energy of the ethical passion that exists. It is one of the most vital factors; as we shall show, the most vital of all. That its efficacy has been invariably overestimated in the past does not alter the fact that it is the element of decisive importance. The chief reason of its failure in the immediate past is that it has been uninstructed. Because it has been uninstructed, it has assumed forms of activity that were really incompatible with the actual social situation. It appealed, for example, in the finest instances, for disinterested ethical passion in a world of men completely incapable of responding to the appeal.

It is this incompatibility of the ethical passion with the objective social situation that was the cause of the supreme tragedy of Jesus. We need not and we do not regret that tragedy.[2] Because it was endured to the end, and not avoided, the type of human perfection was indelibly fixed in the imaginations of men. In the same sense, in 1870, Marx warned the French proletariat against an untimely uprising, against action which was incompatible with the objective situation; nevertheless, when in 1871, the uprising actually took place, Marx hailed the revolutionary initiative of the masses with the utmost enthusiasm, saying that they were 'storming heaven.' It reminds one, pregnantly, of the word of Jesus that the Kingdom of Heaven is taken by violence, and violent men enter into it.

Commenting on this attitude of Marx, Lenin wrote:—

'In this situation, as in so many others, the defeat of a revolutionary onslaught was from the Marxian standpoint of dialectical materialism, from the point of view of the general course and *the outcome* of the proletarian struggle, a lesser evil than would have been a retreat from a position hitherto occupied, a surrender without striking a blow, as such a surrender would have demoralized the proletariat and undermined its readiness for struggle.' (*The Teachings of Karl Marx, by V. I. Lenin, p. 36.*)

The essential purpose of the Marxian doctrine of historical materialism is to put an end, once for all, to the waste of the ethical passion of disinterestedness. Marxism is, and may indeed be defined as, ethical passion come to a full consciousness of itself and its conditions. And that is the reason why Marxism is of crucial importance to-day.

They are blind fools who tell us that ethical passion is dying in the modern world. It is there, pent-up and smouldering, fiercer than ever. Yet it can find no utterance. We are, as individual men, more humane than ever before; yet we feel more impotent than ever before to express our humanity. We look back on history; we see how, blindly but undismayed, mankind has striven in the forms of its noblest individuals to perpetuate the perfection of ethical passion which was established in Jesus. The effort to perpetuate it – to love our neighbour as ourself – is a destiny upon those who are responsive to that organic perfection. Yet the complexity of the modern world appears to deride our efforts. Our consciousness of the difficulties

makes cowards of us. How *can* we make the effort
actual?

To this problem, Marx alone has the answer. He is
the prophet of fully conscious ethical passion; he revealed the form which ethical passion must take if it
is to be appropriate to the knowledge that lies upon
us like a burden, until that appropriateness is understood. He is the prophet of the end of the epoch
which, as an ethical continuity, has its origin in the
supreme example of ethical passion turned tragedy.
For the tragedy of ethical passion has always been
in this: that it has expressed itself in forms of activity
which are discrepant with the objective social situation.
That, we repeat, was never a disaster; the archetypal
tragedy of Jesus was no disaster, because through that
tragedy, and that great man's complete acceptance of
it, the type of disinterestedness was established. It
became a dream in men's minds, a music in their ears,
from which they could never escape. The supreme
form of ethical passion remained real, the significant
variation became established; but the problem of
appropriate action remained unsolved, only to produce
more tragedies.[3] Marx revealed that the time had come
when the form taken by the objective social situation
was such that a truly appropriate action had become
possible. The hour had struck when disinterestedness
could become completely active, when its action was
no longer condemned to incompatibility and inefficacy.

The deep underlying condition of this realization,
in the fully conscious man, was a recognition in some
form or another, of the heterogeneity of Spirit and
Matter. True spirituality had to be finally purified of
contamination. It had to be seen, clearly and distinctly,

that the world of existence was wholly and altogether a material world; and that spirit was a mode of comprehending, *sub specie aeternitatis*, the wholly material world of existence, to which all that is human necessarily belongs. It had to be seen that ethics and social morality, no matter how precious they might be to the individual aflame with ethical and social passion, were wholly human and animal in origin. They had their rise in no transcendental source, and needed no supernatural sanction to maintain themselves. They are, simply and solely, habits of the human animal; but they do not cease to be precious to the human being whose qualities they are, nor to the human race in its groping towards new forms of existence. Values do not cease to be values, because they are not guaranteed by God.

This separation of spirituality and morality involves necessarily, the abolition of what is known as religion, because religion is essentially an amalgam of spirituality and morality, with the proportion of true spirituality diminishing steadily with the process of the years. And this abolition of religion has been proceeding apace in this country, not because of any widespread conscious separation of spirituality and morality, but because of the spread of the simple recognition that the moment had come when morality was taking care of itself. For at least a hundred years the Christian Church has lagged, in effective ethical passion, behind the average of society as a whole. That diluted quantum of the ethic of Jesus which the English Church incorporated had become a common possession. As a repository of ethical values, the Church was obsolete; its power of magical attraction had ceased with the

42

decay of faith in the supernatural, which was at best only a transitory and unsatisfactory symbol of the reality of the spiritual; its social and charitable services, which since it ceased to be Catholic it had performed perfunctorily or not at all, had been organized and established by voluntary non-religious effort, or by the State itself. It endures in England to-day chiefly because it is a corporation, possessing vast properties; its existence is not particularly resented, because in the countryside it still offers a place of meeting and an opportunity of corporate action, because occasionally the parson is the focus of enlightenment, or a pattern of humane behaviour, and because there is still a considerable though dwindling number – a few hundred thousands at most – of people who are believers in the supernatural, and in a life of rewards and punishments after death. We are rightly tolerant enough to hold that their desires should be met and their needs supplied. But the Church, in this country, has become an antiquarian survival.

Thus, the abolition of institutional religion which must follow, in the conscious intelligence, the separation of spirituality and morality, has been accomplished unconsciously in the minds and hearts of the masses. What the conscious intelligence of the nation must achieve is coming to pass instinctively in the body of the nation. There is, in this respect, a harmony between them: in their different orders they have reached the same conclusion with regard to religion. It has ceased to be real.

This correspondence between the unconsciousness and the consciousness of the nation is of the highest significance, for the annihilation of religion as such,

and its complete separation into its heterogeneous
elements of the spiritual and the ethical, is the condition
of the effective expression of ethical passion. For
religion, once the sole channel of such effective
expression of ethical passion as the social situation
permitted, has now become the chief obstacle; its
sole effective function now is to discharge whatever
force of ethical passion comes into contact with it,
into useless and irrelevant activities. In one form or
another – consciously I suppose in the best intelligences
the Church contains, unconsciously in the average of
its ministers – it seeks to perpetuate the equivocation
by which awareness of the spiritual has for its corollary
indifference to the material. This equivocation is now
exposed by the conscious and spiritual intelligence
of the few and rejected by the instinctive ethical judgment of the many.

This double preparation is necessary for the real
advent of the Marxian revolution, in forms appropriate
to this country. I insist upon the latter qualification.
An intelligent understanding of Marxism is extra-
ordinarily rare in this country. It is associated,
enthusiastically by a minority, with genuine horror by a
majority, with bloody revolution. Neither side has
enough genuine acquaintance with Marxism to understand that the instinctive shrinking from a bloody
revolution in this country is a factor in the objective
situation which a true Marxian must take into account.
The 'bourgeoisification' of the English proletariat is
a reality, purely deplorable to the rigid Marxist of
the Russian type, but to the more flexible Marxist,
who is not enamoured of bloodshed for its own sake,
it has an admirable side. Every country will get the

Marxism it deserves, as Russia did; and we English may thank our stars, our long economic monopoly and our basic political good sense as well, that we have in fact deserved a better Marxism than any other nation in the world. We must try to get it. We also shall 'expropriate the expropriators,' but it is possible that we may do it more gently than our Russian brothers.

Our opportunity is indeed prodigious. I write these words immediately after the result of the General Election has been declared. It shows that even a divided Labour Party, hopelessly misled by inefficient leaders, fighting on a false issue, can yet muster behind it one-third of the total electorate. That is to say that the irreducible minimum of active supporters of the Labour Party in this country is one-third of the population. Within ten years from now it is almost certain that the Labour Party will come into full power in this country. In that time its task is to find a real faith. Hitherto it has had none. It has been content to live parasitically upon the capitalist system, and even in the matter of its leaders it has been content to accept a large number of men with no creed, no conviction, and no disinterestedness. Its period of eclipse is the time when it can set itself in order, and become compact, coherent, and unashamedly revolutionary. We English who proudly date our modern political period from the Great Revolution, have no cause to be afraid of the word 'revolution.' We can produce our own, and we can, if we will, see to it that the next one shall be like the last one – a pattern to the world.[4]

The practical task before the Labour Party is simply to convert one third of the electorate (and also itself) to the recognition of the fact that stares them in the face – that the system of individualistic capitalism is doomed. It does not function effectively any more. It must be replaced by another system, and that other system must be non-individualistic. Mitigated individualism will not do; by sheer force of circumstances, even a National Government will find itself driven to mitigate individualism still more and more, and still it will not do. There will be more world-crises, each more devastating than the last, until either our individualism has been imperceptibly mitigated into non-existence, or we see that a deliberate act of abolition is necessary. The party of the future will be the party that has, consciously in the few, unconsciously in the many, accepted and achieved the Marxian revolution.

One condition of this is the rejection of religion. The practical rejection of religion is sufficient for the rank and file; but the conscious and deliberate rejection of it is required of the conscious. For this is the only means by which the ethical passion which, in spite of all appearances, is more plentiful than ever, can be made completely effective. The rejection of religion, it may be said, is a *fait accompli*. In the purely negative sense of such a rejection the statement might be plausible. In fact, even in that sense it is not true. One at least of the true intellectual leaders of this generation has deliberately returned to the Church. But what is required is the deliberate and positive rejection of religion, *in a religious act*, by the complete dissociation of the spiritual and the ethical-political. This cannot happen of itself. It is not enough, for instance, that those whose interests are primarily social should practically and unreflectingly ignore the spiritual; for to ignore the spiritual is to restrict one's capacity for complete devotion of the self which the situation requires. It is to leave the door open for the personal factor to enter in and contaminate the purity of our ethical materialism.

What is demanded of the conscious minority is a positive and dynamic rejection of religion. For them a merely negative lapse from religion is not merely insufficient, it is disastrous – ethically and politically. It leads to moral dilettantism and to coquetting with the empty and barren idea of Fascism.[5] For the difference between a lapse from religion and a dynamic rejection of religion is tremendous. To reject, unconsciously, a manifestation of human life so ancient, so venerable, so evidently the vehicle of precious human values, as the Christian religion is an offence against human responsibility; it proceeds from weary ignorance. Far better than such neglect, is the deliberate determination to return to the Christian orthodoxy. That also proceeds from weariness, but it proceeds also from knowledge. The objection to this return to Christianity is simple; it is that weariness has been allowed to turn knowledge aside from its own full consummation. It is a sinking down in exhaustion half way on the path of self-annihilation. For the conscious acceptance of the Christian religion to-day does veritably require an act of self-annihilation. And that is good: that is dynamic. But by the return to orthodox Christianity this vital and vivifying act of self-annihilation is aborted; the form of the new man is predetermined, and therefore he is not new. In other words, such backward-turning spirits seek, no doubt unconsciously, to combine self-annihilation with safety. It is not possible. It means

47

that they have kept back from the holocaust of self that is required of them, an invincible core of self-hood. They have failed at the test.

But there is this to be said. They have at least seen and known that there was a test to be endured; they have had the sense that 'this night is thy life required of thee,' that real *sacrifice* is demanded of this generation. What they have not seen and known, or rather what they have not obscurely but securely felt, is that each crucial generation of men has its own peculiar destiny of sacrifice – a form of sacrifice possible to and there-fore demanded of, it alone. To return to a past pattern of sacrifice is to shrink from *the* sacrifice. For *the* sacrifice must always be a dedication of oneself to the unknown. To know the issue is to have withdrawn from the sacrifice: to have chosen the past, and denied the future.

Not then to lapse from religion, not to return to religion, but dynamically to reject religion is required. That is to say, we must know that which we reject; that is to say, we must recognize and be responsive to the values which have been embodied in religion; that is to say, we must be determined to perpetuate those values in ourselves. Those values, objectively distin-guished, are two: Spirituality and Disinterestedness – an impersonal awareness of Eternity, and a personal consecration to ethical passion in Time. Those values were embodied in the living figure of a new Man, the son of Man, according to the circumstances of his time. Our duty is to embody them, as far as we may, accord-ing to the circumstances of our time.

48

BOURGEOIS AND PROLETARIAN

ONCE, not so many years ago, I was nearly penniless. My wife was very ill, I had nothing but my pen to keep us, and I could sell very little of what that pen produced. The fifty pounds I have saved against the rainy day began to dwindle, till at last it became less than ten. Then I began to be gnawed by incessant anxiety, and I suppose my anxiety showed on my face, so as to be obvious to a charming woman-friend of mine with whom I was taking tea. She asked me: 'Was I worried?' After some pressing, I admitted that I was. 'Not about money?' she said incredulously. 'Yes, about money.' She replied, vivaciously:

'Oh, *never* worry about money. It's a waste of life. Never worry if you can't live on your income. *Sell your securities.*'

For a moment I was simply nonplussed. Then I had the impulse to tell her that I had never had more than fifty pounds in the bank in my life: and, as for possessing a 'security,' I had never so much as seen one. But I restrained the impulse, because it would be embarrassing to us both. She would feel under the compulsion to offer to lend me money – I should feel that I had placed her under the compulsion. So I appeared to take her advice seriously, and we parted good friends – as good friends as might be, who must needs shake hands across a vast.

In that encounter, the meaning of the word 'security'

was impressed upon my brain. I meditated on it. It seemed to me that the world was divided into those who possessed securities – of which the 'securities' she spoke of are the perfected modern form – and those who had none. And the abyss between them was the same old abyss that divided Dives from Lazarus. Moreover, I was puzzled by the fact that my friend assumed, so simply and so evidently without need of question, that I belonged to the security-possessing class. At last it dawned on me that, because I was an educated person, who had gone through the established process of gentleman-production by way of a public school and the university, she had always assumed without question that I possessed the economic appurtenances of the 'gentleman.' Further, it dawned on me that she was justified in the assumption, because I was what was at that time a comparatively rare phenomenon – a board-school boy who, by dint of a lucky scholarship at the age of nine, had been thrust neck and crop into the machine for gentleman-production. I looked like the thing she had assumed I was. How could she guess that I was an economic sham? I was, in fact, a proletarian in bourgeois clothing.

For this distinction between the security-possessing class and the class of people which possesses none roughly corresponds to the essential distinction between the bourgeoisie and the proletariat as drawn by Karl Marx. Security, in the modern world, is almost synonymous with 'securities' – for 'securities,' whatever form they take – whether the title-deeds to landed property or a share-certificate in a company – denote some form of ownership of the means of production. Nor is this fundamental property of the security-possessing class really affected by the evident presence of yet another class which, though not possessing 'securities' in any obvious form, yet possesses security – the great modern class of state-servants or salaried functionaries, who are not liable to discharge, and are liable to pension. For their privilege of security ultimately depends on the fact that, by virtue of its powers of taxation, the State (or a great corporation like the Church) is the chief owner of the means of production. The State is, as it were, the holder of first debentures in every enterprise: so that the pension of the municipal dustman or the High Court Judge ultimately denotes a life-interest in the means of production, a life-charge on the surplus-value created by human labour.

The distinction is absolute in theory, not in fact. Economically speaking, a large number of proletarians – though far fewer than is generally urged – have a streak of bourgeois in their economic composition: they have small savings bearing interest, and in so far as in England they come under Unemployment Insurance as hitherto conducted, they partake, in some pitiful degree, of the nature of state-employees. And again there are many proletarians born who have got some distance along the way to becoming full-fledged bourgeois. This is the form necessarily taken by the individual's struggle towards economic security in the modern world. To achieve it, wholly or in part, he must become, in the large sense of the word, a 'property-owner' in some form; he must establish a valid claim, by some means or other, to be maintained by the labour of others. The only way of doing this, in the modern world, is to acquire directly or indirectly a share in the necessary means of production.

Yet the claim of the individual to be maintained by the labour of others is not in itself monstrous. First, it is not monstrous when it is seen to be the fact that only by establishing such a claim, in the modern condition of society, can the individual achieve economic security: which we must admit to be a legitimate and necessary aim. Second, it is not monstrous – on the contrary – that a man who has done his share of the productive labour of society, should be honourably maintained by the labour of others when his capacity for useful labour fails; or that a man who is willing and able to do his share should be honourably maintained when there is no work for him to do. In any decently organized society these two claims would be admitted to the full. They have only to be stated to command our instant assent as ethical beings.

Yet, in fact, what do we see? We see that the claim of the poor man, who is willing and able to work, to be maintained at a bare subsistence-minimum when there is no work for him to do, is grudgingly admitted by some, and hotly resented by others. And we see that the reason for this grudging admission and this hot resentment is that the satisfaction of the poor man's claim, in the present condition of society, would endanger the economic security of the rich man. We see also that what the rich man conceives to be his necessary degree of economic security is utterly disproportionate to the economic security claimed by the poor man. The poor man simply claims to be barely maintained when, for no fault of his own, he cannot work; the rich man claims to be maintained, in comfort or in luxury, even if he does no work at all. And because the poor man's claim promises to make inroads upon the claim of the rich man, it is at best grudgingly conceded to superior force, or passionately combated.

It seems sheer madness to a lucid interrogation. Yet there it is, and being so, it is so of necessity. We must understand the necessity. Why cannot the rich man simply admit that the poor man's claim is just and *must* be satisfied? It must be manifest to him as an ethical being. It must indeed. But unfortunately he is is not an ethical being. As Jesus remarked, it is harder for a camel to go through the eye of a needle than for a rich man to enter into the kingdom of God. It is true that for nearly two thousand years the Church has been resolutely engaged in assuring him that on this point in particular Jesus was mistaken; and, quite naturally, the rich man has laid the flattering unction to his soul. But the Church as a body has never, at any time, known, or cared to know, what Jesus meant by the kingdom of God. This again quite naturally: because as Jesus said so plainly, the kingdom of God was a condition into which it was incredibly difficult for a rich man to enter. That would never do. And yet Jesus meant what he said, and it was true. For the kingdom of God is simply the condition of an ethical being, the state of disinterestedness.[6]

And – nineteen hundred years have proved it – it *is* about as easy for a camel to go through the eye of a needle as for a rich man to be disinterested. I am not accusing the rich men as a class; nor do I use the term 'rich' as it is commonly used. It means, in this context, all those who enjoy some real degree of economic security. I myself, for instance, in the eyes of the truly rich man, am almost an example of poverty. With luck I earn £600 a year, and I have about £150 a year which I do not earn besides. But in this context I am quite definitely a rich man, even though my small degree of economic security has been laboriously acquired. But I know, in my own case, how long and difficult has been the struggle towards some shadow of disinterestedness; and I can well understand how much more difficult must be the struggle of those who have been bred in an atmosphere of complete economic security.

We cannot blame the rich for not being disinterested. But neither can we wait for them to become disinterested. We shall wait till doomsday for the camels to go through the needle's eye of their own accord. And that is the answer to those (of whom I once was one) who bid us wait for the 'change of heart' in men before we attempt to change society radically. Nor need we wait: for the problem is not what it at first sight seems to be. The problem is not to create a majority of men who, by painful stages, have reached a point of veritable disinterestedness. These must always be relatively few, and were we to wait for them to become a majority, we should wait for ever. The problem is vastly simplified by the fact that there is in existence a great body of men, who may at any time become an actual majority in this country, whose interests make the same demand upon society as our disinterestedness.

We need not, indeed it is vitally important that we should not, indulge in any illusions whatever about the proletariat. To require disinterestedness from it, as a class, is fantastic. We ought to be astonished that so many of them have attained a level of disinterestedness which puts ours to shame. What we have to see, and to see clearly, is that our disinterestedness imperatively requires that we should identify ourselves with the interests of the working class. And the completeness of that identification will be, in itself, a test of the reality of our disinterestedness. Precisely because the proletariat is not, and cannot be, animated in the mass by the same motives as ourselves; precisely because, judged in the purely ethical order, it is to some extent animated by the same kind of interests as the class to which it is opposed – this act of identification becomes a test of the reality of our disinterestedness.

Real identification with the proletariat involves real incorporation with it. It thus involves, in the world of existence, a definite sacrifice of the ego. Apart from the fact that the instinctive aim of the proletariat, to which we adhere, involves the complete economic sacrifice of ourselves, we are committed, in making the final and necessary decision to incorporate ourselves with the proletariat, to the sacrifice of our most precious values in so far as we ourselves do not directly embody them. In other words, our culture is really irrelevant to the movement to which we deliberately devote ourselves. In the world of the proletariat into which we enter we have not a shadow of right to expect such qualities as respect for the autonomy of art or spirituality. If we find them at all, then we must be grateful as for a gift to which we have no rightful claim. But our true and appropriate attitude of mind will be one which can never be disappointed: it is the attitude which clearly conceives that the values of our culture, however precious they may be, are required in strictness to be completely sacrificed. They are part of the ego which has to be annihilated. No doubt it would be perverse, and wantonly destructive, in ourselves to make this sacrifice where it is not actually demanded by the movement to which we are dedicated. But, at the best, much sacrifice in this respect will be demanded of us; we must have been prepared to sacrifice even more.

But the test of our disinterestedness will have been made before this. For disinterestedness, as we have seen, is a many-sided virtue. The first claim it makes upon us is that we should see things as they are. We cannot see things as they are in the world of Matter except at the price of self-annihilation. That, and nothing less, is required by the disinterested seeing of the actual situation. We cannot see it thus unless we have become detached from our own interests. It is the veil interposed by our instinctive attachment to our own interests which makes us see things wholly awry. We, the relatively rich, assume that it is a necessary part of the scheme of things that there should be mighty distinctions between classes, based on a mighty discrepancy between their economic positions. Or if we profess, almost always with evident insincerity, to have an open mind on this matter, we surreptitiously indulge our interests by a great parade of our concern with the advantages that accrue to the social organism by the maintenance of variety. For this variety with which we discover ourselves to be passionately concerned always turns out to be variety of the kind that demands economic inequality. As though there would not be as much variety in a society in which a fundamental economic equality were enforced. True, it would not be the same variety. Certain social types would perish – types to some of which we can sincerely accord attractiveness and social value. But social types have perished before in the stress of economic change, and they must continue to perish. The nation did not go into mourning over the destruction of the old handicraftsman, who was at least as valuable a type as the average modern aristoplutocrat. (And, after all, there is no reason why in the future State there should not be a sort of Yellowstone Park for the accommodation and exhibition of some of the more striking varieties of modern Anglo-Saxon). It is quite conceivable, too, that the type which we ourselves may be said to represent – the 'intellectuals' who have perhaps learned their disinterestedness through their fragmentary opportunities of economic freedom – will not survive. It cannot be helped. But it is not wholly accidental to the purpose of this book that it may teach some of these how to endow themselves with a survival value. For there is only one way – to be ready to sacrifice their all. By that readiness they will have earned the right to survive; in virtue of that readiness, if they see no prospect of surviving, they will not care.

In every detail the necessity of self-annihilation awaits us. We have to purify ourselves completely of ourselves that we may see what the situation demands. To cling to the past, in any shape or form, is forbidden. That of the past which *lives*, is living in ourselves. The past to which we feel the need to cling as to something other and more solid than ourselves is the dead past. It can breed only contamination and corruption. No matter how noble and precious it appears, no matter how noble and precious in our own eyes is that element in ourselves to which it appeals, we shall find that in so far as it serves to hold us back from a complete surrender of ourselves to the Communist ideal of utter disinterestedness it is the mask of interest, not the vehicle of value.

THE PATTERN OF HISTORY

BUT why, it may be asked, is this required of us now and not before? If this is necessary now, why was it not necessary a generation or two generations ago?

The answer to this question has been implicit in this book. The moment has arrived when we must make it as explicit as we can. This we shall attempt to do, as it were, in descending levels until we finally reach the level of immediate and practical policy.

The ethical passion of disinterestedness, I believe, first emerged in the evolution of human history in the Jewish prophets. By a process of projection, the new impulse of the human animal was credited to God, who was conceived as demanding the new ethical sensitiveness which was emerging.[7] In Jesus this ethical sensitiveness reached a consummation; it now completely outran the contemporary capacities of the Jewish race – a 'material' situation which was religiously expressed in the propagation by Jesus of an incomprehensible conception of God, as a loving and completely forgiving Father of prodigal humanity – and ethically expressed in the paradoxical morality of non-resistance to evil. This ethic of non-resistance was perfectly appropriate to the objective situation, for the recalcitrance of the 'material' environment (men and women capable at most of a purely personal response to Jesus) was then insuperable. There is not the faintest external evidence that Jesus contemplated or countenanced armed rebellion, and the internal evidence of his doctrine and his sayings is almost wholly against it. Jesus appears to have been a complete realist with regard to the Roman power – 'Render unto Caesar the things that are Caesar's.' Thus both in regard to the religious conceptions, and to the national ethical tradition of armed rebellion, Jesus appeared an apostate and a traitor. He was, within the circumstances of his time, a completely revolutionary spirit. The fundamental rightness of his estimation of those circumstances was revealed in the catastrophe that overtook national Judaism a little while after his death. Whereas he, aiming at and achieving a merely individual crucifixion, fixed the ideal of disinterestedness in the consciousness of Western humanity for the whole epoch to which we belong, national Judaism crucified the Jewish race, in vain.

On one level – that of immediate effectiveness – we may regard the tragedy of Jesus as the supreme example of the waste of ethical passion; on another level, that of final efficacy, it is the perfect example of the potency of complete disinterestedness. Jesus, by his utter disinterestedness, religiously expressed in 'Father, nevertheless not as I will, but as thou wilt,' became the pure instrument of human destiny, the perfect seed of future human perfection. He became the leaven that leaveneth the whole lump of Western humanity.

This constant pattern of disinterestedness present to the Western consciousness has been dynamic in its potency. It gave form to an organized civilization – the international civilization of Catholicism – which represented the maximum possible of disinterestedness compatible with the then economic situation. Probably there has never yet been a nearer approach to basic equality of opportunity for the individual, and real internationalism, than in the medieval Church in its prime. None the less the objective expression of this advanced ideal was economically parasitic in the world of men; it took place within a charmed circle, within a section of the world fenced off from economic immediacy by privilege based on interestedness. For the economic privilege as against the world without, which was the condition of the actual equality and internationalism within the Church, was extorted by the appeal of supernatural authority to those who believed in it. Finally, owing to the decay of controlling belief within the Church, the position of economic privilege was monstrously abused, and owing to the decay of belief outside the Church the intolerable abuse could be actively resented. The collapse of the Catholic system had begun. In England the Church was expropriated, by men who had not as individuals the faintest ethical superiority over those whom they expropriated, but who had the impersonal justification of being instruments of economic destiny. In France the same necessary act of expropriation of the Church was delayed until 1789; in Russia till 1917; in Spain until this present year, 1931. The secularization of this, the last *really* Catholic country in Europe, – i.e. largely Catholic in its economic organization – marks the close of an epoch: the final collapse, in the conflict with economic reality, of the first effort to mould society on the inspiration of Jesus.

Meanwhile, the quasi-spiritual but wholly 'material' influence of Jesus had been at work in individuals.

Here it suffered less of the distortion that was inevitable in a society moving towards capitalistic production. Whereas on the one hand the impulse to economic individualism had been finally liberated by the collapse of the Catholic system, which had claimed to regulate the economic conduct of individuals as a matter of morality, on the other hand the free growth of economic individualism began to make the profession of Christianity an evident hypocrisy.[8] Thus there arose a form of Christianity which made its religion the concern of the individual soul alone, and disinterested itself completely in the economic conduct of man. This form of Christianity (of which past Quakerism is the perfect type) produced a few notable saints, and a swarm of hypocrites, convinced of their own superior morality in frowning upon all humane enjoyments which distracted them from the pursuit of wealth.[9]

For the individuals genuinely responsive to the ethical perfection of Jesus the conflict and the struggle in this period (in England roughly from the Reformation to the First Reform Bill) were extreme. In so far as they did not succeed in drugging themselves by the pursuit of good works which were to a more comprehensive vision condemned to futility, their only resource was some form of Quietism. Good works were evidently condemned to futility: for they were inspired by a religion which did not and indeed could not concern itself with the economic individualism of society; whereas that economic process, over which religion had and claimed no control, inevitably created, as a constant by-product, the misery and crime which the good works sought, in vain, to mitigate. There is a fearful pathos in the spectacle of Elizabeth Fry labouring her life to reform prisons into which were emptied the human wreckage of the economic process which her particular religion not only condoned but directly stimulated. As Christianity in its corporate and Catholic form collapsed under the surge of economic individualism, so Christianity, in its individualistic and Protestant form, was caught in a vicious circle. It ended by giving ethical fervour to the most inhuman oppression the world had known – the massacre of the workers under early English industrialism. Then arose the last in the succession of the great Jewish prophets – Karl Marx – a man of the race which, above all others, had known the iniquity of oppression, and wakened the soul of the world against it.

But what had happened to make of economic individualism so inhuman a Moloch? Nothing but the constantly accelerating process by which the nation passed from being a rudimentary and almost anarchic economic combination into an intricate economic organism. The new network of communication was as a new system of blood-circulation to the hitherto unorganized body. Whereas previously its parts had existed in virtual dislocation, so that there was but a rudimentary exchange of commodities, now these flowed fast and free. Steam which conveyed them at unheard-of speed, produced them in unheard-of quantities. Local isolation, and local limitation, were no more. The machine had made not a mechanism, but an organism of this country. Suddenly the menace of economic individualism was revealed. Men were not worse than they had been before: the new order of industrial capitalists was not, ethically speaking, a new

63

race of criminals. Hence the delay in getting even the flimsiest measures to control them on to the statute-book. They were simply doing what men had always done – what they would with their own. But the new machinery of social production had immeasurably magnified the consequences of their instinctive individualist action. What had hitherto been mainly a conflict within the individual was revealed as a cleavage in society. The conflict in the individual was the conflict between self-interest and the ethical impulse. Interest indeed almost invariably won, but its victory was mitigated to some extent in the anarchic local economy, by the close human contact between master and man which was one aspect of local isolation. It was not until the machine on the one hand had broken down the barriers which had hitherto prevented the nation from becoming an economic unity, and on the other immeasurably multiplied the products of human labour, that the real nature and final outcome of competitive individualism was made plain. But not to every eye.

What many men did see was the unheard-of misery of the labouring class under the new dispensation. What many men did see was that it was 'inevitable.' But the word 'inevitable' applied to a condition of human society has, alas, two distinct meanings according to the penetration and disinterestedness of the man who uses it. It is one thing to see that the creation of human misery is a necessary consequence of the economic system that obtains, and that that system itself is a necessary phase of the evolution of society. It is quite another thing to see that chief among the conditions which combined to produce that maleficent organization of society – conditions which, because they objectively existed, were necessary – was the ignorance and interestedness of human beings. However necessary a given condition of human society may be, the fact remains that it is human beings who have made it.[10] In other words, though it is indeed inevitable that human beings should be what they are, it is not inevitable that they should continue to be what they are: though it is necessary that human society should be what it is, it is not necessary that it should remain what it is. On the contrary, the possibility of change in the human being is ethically self-evident, and historically demontrable. The history of human society is the history of constant change.

But who, save an unreasoning optimist, could have expected the change that was required? For it was required that the human individual should cease to be driven by economic self-interest; and far more than this was required. It was required that a majority of the human individuals in this country should cease to be animated consciously or unconsciously by economic self-interest. The demand was fantastic and exorbitant. At best a few thousand chosen individuals, after years of experience, might achieve this pure disinterestedness; they would be economically powerless against the majority. For it is utterly mistaken to suppose, as do some well-meaning 'spiritualists,' that disinterestedness propagates itself in some transcendental fashion, and that the ethical passion of individuals can change the world. That is the millenarian illusion, from which it is high time that the human consciousness was purged once for all. Ethical passion, to be effective, must await an objective situation appropriate to itself.

And Marx, and Marx alone, with profound prophetic insight, saw that this crucial moment in human history had arrived. A situation had at last arisen in which human self-interest must inevitably create its own antithesis. The blind struggle of the individual after his own advantage had become magnified and changed in the new mechanic dispensation of capitalism, into the blind struggle of the social organism against itself. The vital conflict had passed from individuals to the system: the master had become a class, the man had become a class. And those two classes were inevitably arrayed against one another. There were good masters still; still there were loyal men. But the vital emphasis lay not in the master's goodness, nor in the man's loyalty, but in the fact that the master inevitably belonged to the exploiting, the man to the exploited class. For, under the new capitalist dispensation, if the master was determined to be good – i.e. to treat his men as human beings – he was bound to go under in the competitive struggle, and the last state of his men would be worse than the first. For only by making profits could he produce or attract more capital, and only by producing or attracting more capital could he keep pace with the improvements in technique. He must make profits, and he must make large profits; it was his function in the system. And that could only be done by one of two things: either by keeping the wages of his men at a minimum, or (the principle of 'enlightened' capitalism, typified by Mr. Henry Ford) by bringing his technical efficiency to a competitive maximum, and so increasing production per labour unit that the prime cost of the product was so low that it enabled him at once to pay higher wages to his workers and to undersell his competitors. But this was a merely specious solution of the problem; for if we consider the world as a whole, this underselling of competitors merely resulted in misery in another part of the world-system. The same process of mechanisation which had made the nation a single economic organism, had made an economic organism of the whole world. The Detroit worker prospered, the worker in Coventry was discharged.

VII

CAPITALISM AS WORLD-SUICIDE

WHAT does it matter to us, it might have been said, twenty years ago, if England prospers, and the whole world perishes? To-day, even though a majority of Englishmen may believe it in their simple hearts, the faith is cracking. We are beginning to feel, though not to understand, that if the whole world perishes, we perish too. We as a nation are experiencing the feelings of the poor devil in the early days of industrialism who was thrown out of work by the machine, and some are tempted into his naive reactions: they want to smash it.[11] It is not the machine that is the devil; simply that the men who control it are fools. And it is terribly hard for any of us not to be fools nowadays, because our vision is not adjusted to the new scale of reality. We cannot get it into our minds that the nation is now one unitary social organism; how can we get it into our minds that the world also is a single economic organism composed of many nations? We cannot think in those terms. So we vaguely and feebly wait for the new wave of prosperity which will lift the world out of the slough of depression. It has happened before, we say, and it is bound to happen again. There is a slump; then comes a boom. But we forget that something happened between the last slump and this one, and that was something that never had happened before – the great and inevitable war of 1914–1918. Leaving utterly aside as of no consequence the sheer outrage on humanity – most of the men who felt it an outrage were killed in it, anyhow; leaving utterly aside as of no consequence the appalling waste of the finest human life, of the past and future riches of the world – leaving these things utterly aside, let us consider these two consequences of the war alone. First, that it gave hitherto unprecedented impetus to the mechanization and rationalization of industry: as a direct consequence of the war-demands the technique of industry was immeasurably improved, and thus the coherence of the national and international economic organisms immeasurably intensified. Second, that it gave an equal and opposite impetus to the process of national exclusiveness, that it increased the number of independent sectarian states, determined to flourish at the expense of their neighbours. At a moment when, in the world of economic reality, the barriers between nations had been broken down, at that moment in the world of political fiction the racial separation of nations was made complete. Consider those two consequences of the war. They explain the slump, but they do not explain how it will pass away of itself. On the contrary they show plainly that it will not pass away of itself, any more than the misery produced by capitalism in the national organism will pass away by itself. If it is allowed to pass away by itself, God help us: for it will pass away through famine and tribulation and pestilence.

Do not imagine that I suggest, as Mr. Wells suggests, that we have only to think in world-terms to find the cure. I do not believe it is possible to cure the sickness of the world in that way. Bourgeois idealists – like Mr.

Wells – distract themselves from the necessary atten-
tion to their own private house, by concentrating
indignation on the world at large. Their indignation
is sincere, in the sense that they are really indignant.
But that kind of sincerity is of no use in the world any
more. It is self-deception. Mr. Wells does not know
he is deceiving himself, and he will resent it hotly
when I say so. Nevertheless, that is what, in the actual
world-situation, his bourgeois internationalism really is.
Internationalism begins at home; it begins, for the
individual who is not simply a member of the actual
proletariat, by a ruthless sacrifice of the ego. And of
this Mr. Wells is apparently incapable. He has always
wanted a world-revolution without a moral revolution
in himself. And that for the intelligentsia is *fatal*. Such
a man cannot be a Communist on the surface – which
is what Mr. Wells's internationalism amounts to – and
be bourgeois underneath.[12] He *can* do it, of course; Mr.
Wells does it. Practically every middle-class member of
the Labour Party in this country does it; but only at
the price of a fundamental self-deception, and often
also of a manifest insincerity. They talk glibly, but
the voice *sounds* wrong. Universalize Mr. Wells,
magnify him, after the same fashion as capitalist
economy has magnified the egoism of the individual,
and you get the world that is now. Not a different
world, as Mr. Wells would like to persuade himself, and
to make us believe. A world of *efficient* capitalism –
which is what Mr. Wells desires – is a contradiction
in terms. The fact that it is the ideal of the enlightened
bourgeois to-day, that it is the aim of the present
National Government in England, does not alter the
simple truth. Rationalize industry to the uttermost,

cover the country with works as efficient as Mr. Henry Ford's at Detroit, imagine (if you can) England restored to an optimum of economic prosperity, it will be paid for by a pessimum of oppression and misery elsewhere. And though for a few more years we may succeed in hiding our heads in the sand, and in persuading ourselves that the misery and poverty of those other parts of the world-organism do not concern us, we shall discover, once more to our astonishment and dismay, that disease in the foot affects the heart of the great body of which we are now the ignorant parts. There will be no one to buy the magnificent and multitudinous products of our efficient capitalism. We shall have to go to war to secure to ourselves a monopoly market; and even if we are 'victorious' – 'victorious' again – within the closed market we have secured we shall enact the same inevitable catastrophe.

The world to-day has reached a climacteric. Dimly we feel it, obscurely we know it. The wise men shake their heads. They know that something is radically wrong. But their ointments would only skin the wound, the festering beneath would rage on unchecked. If only, they say, the world would agree to stabilize world-prices; if only America and France would learn to play the game of the gold-standard; if only France would cease to stand upon the letter of her bond with Germany – then the world would run on wheels again. Alas, it is not true. Leaving aside the fact that in all these remedies we are asking for something that, under the system to which all nations belong, cannot be given; for we are asking that people should lend their money where they *know* it is not secure, that they should cease to be competitive in their interests of their – now less fortunate – competitors; that they should abrogate 'the sanctity of contract' in order that future contracts may be sanctified; leaving aside, in short, the fact that our remedies ask the impossible, the truth is that if they were to be applied, the only result would be an armistice during which the economic antagonists throughout the world would prepare to hurl themselves into a last desperate conflict. For even if, by a stretch of imagination which no sane man can compass, a whole series of international agreements were concluded, abolishing tariffs, delimiting economic spheres of influence, establishing the maximum of efficiency in international arrangements, the arrangement would be denounced within a year, unless it were simultaneously enacted that the competitive system must cease *within* the nations as well. For as things are, industrialized nations can only 'prosper' by selling more and more of their products abroad. That necessity can only be overcome by the internal abolition of the capitalist system. Efficient capitalism means one thing – and one thing only – the mobilization of the entire resources of the world for a final and completely devastating war. This is the naked meaning of the statement that efficient capitalism is a contradiction in terms. Capitalism, ultimately, can only magnify on a colossal scale the conflict that is inherent in it as a mode of production. It can only enlarge the cut-throat competition that obtains between individual enterprises into cut-throat competition between nations or groups of nations. You can stop the fatal process at the source, or not at all.

VIII

THE ONLY REMEDY

INTERNATIONALISM can only be created by the super-session of individualism in the nations. And how can individualism in the nations be superseded? If the answer were that individualism in the nations could only be superseded by the supersession of individualism in the hearts of a majority of the individuals that compose them, then indeed there would be nothing to do but to sit down and await the catastrophe. If again the answer were, as most critics of Marxism and many so-called Marxists affect to believe, that the supersession of individualism in the nations will come about inevitably by the mere extension and intensification of the capitalist process, by the necessary increase of the proletariat in numbers and in power until the overthrow of the bourgeoisie is a natural consummation, then again there would be nothing to do but to sit down and await the millennium, *which, alas, would be indistinguishable from the aforesaid catastrophe. It would be exactly the same objective event, looked at from the other side. For us who have to come to the future from the present, the inevitable millennium would be the inevitable catastrophe.*

What we have to do is to expedite the historically necessary process in which we are involved. The objective situation is this. Within the national organism are the two essential classes, bourgeois and prole-tariat, instinctively united in themselves, and instinc-tively arrayed against one another. Left to itself, the result of the conflict between these opposing elements will be the 'victory' of the proletariat. That is indeed inevitable. But the 'victory' will be abstract; in actual fact the 'victory' will take the form of economic collapse, with misery and starvation in its train. It will be a 'victory' in which every one, proletarian and bourgeois alike, will suffer, for it will be a 'victory' only in the sense that it will be a crucial moment of transition out of which will emerge a social order in which the relative position of the hostile elements has been transposed. Therefore it is not the 'victory' which really concerns us as humane beings: for that will come, whether we will or no. What concerns us is the nature and quality and duration of the 'moment' – which may be measured in years – of the transition.

Somehow, we have to secure humane control of that 'moment.' And the condition of securing control of that 'moment' is, first, to see clearly that it is bound to come; we cannot control an event for which we are unprepared. Second, we have to see clearly how, and by what means, it can be controlled. This is not the occasion to enter into the kind of military details beloved by our naive Nazis, or our naive Communists, dressed all in Russian leather; we are concerned with the elucidation of fundamental principles. And the chief of these fundamental principles is that we must resolve to be on the winning side. No one who has read this book so far will accuse me of the deadly sin of political opportunism. Nevertheless, I say bluntly that the fundamental condition of conscious control of the transition 'moment' is that those to whom this book is addressed, those who are in any way capable of responding to its arguments and its appeal, *must resolve to be on the winning side.* First, because it must win; second, because it ought to win; and third, because this resolve is the necessary condition of humane control during the crucial transition moment. In this decisive resolve, the demands of political realism and the demands of ethical passion are at one.

Our duty to be disinterested – our duty to be on the winning side? I am not writing for fools; still less for reactionary chop-logics. That these two things are not in the least antagonistic in reality, though they conflict in verbal expression, will have become evident by now. Still, we may insist again on the vital point that for *us* to resolve, as we must, to be on the winning side demands all the disinterestedness of which we are likely to be capable. We have to have achieved a first disinterestedness in order to see that the situation is what it actually is – one that can no longer be plastered and tinkered into a semblance of health, that it is one that is moving, with an acceleration that dumbs our imagination, to the catastrophe – or the millennium; in order to see that, in spite of all the social cross-divisions and varieties produced by our relatively ancient system of capitalism and our relatively elastic political organization, still the elemental class-war exists and is the fundamental reality of our present English situation; in order to see that we have to choose, and to choose now – bourgeois or proletariat? We need a second disinterestedness if our choice is to be real. For we – I mean the majority of those who will read this book – are bourgeois. We have an accumulation of bourgeois values, which are genuinely precious – refinements of art, of social conduct, created

75

by centuries out of the leisure secured to the non-productive classes by the productive. These are good things, and we know that they are good. It will be a pain to us to part with them. It may be that we shall not have to part with them altogether; but it is certain that if we cling to them, we shall fail in the disinterestedness that the situation requires of us. We can be sure of carrying into the future only those past values which are actually incorporated in our living selves. If we insist on travelling with luggage, we shall assuredly lose the train. We must be prepared to take the plunge naked or not at all.

It is the refusal of this destiny of nakedness which has vitiated the leadership of the working-classes in this country. Very, very few of their leaders have faced the necessity of radical sacrifice, or of a basic asceticism. Socially, even the leader born of the working-classes, becomes bourgeois: he becomes a politician among politicians. And those bourgeois politicians who condescend to take the plums of office in a Labour government are largely careerists of the familiar kind. This is the especial danger which confronts the radical Labour Movement in this country: unconsciously and inevitably it accepts the forms, and with them the spirit, of the past. It has ceased to be, what it was in the days of the Chartists – *revolutionary*. Our position of economic privilege during the nineteenth century, our monopoly in industrial technique and our consequent prosperity, have combined with our monopoly of workable Parliamentary government, to induce the feeling that *our* revolution must be gradual, until this feeling is become an ineradicable conviction. The conviction of gradualness and security remains, but the economic monopoly which was its basis and justification is gone. This creates a peculiarly deceptive and dangerous situation, in which the necessity for a clear conception of the goal and a resolute advance towards it is lost. Labour has forgotten how to be radical. That should be, to the realist, a cause not of self-gratulation, but of misgiving. For radical solutions are now more than ever necessary, and the only means of applying them is through the Labour movement. In other words, it is even a *national* necessity that the Labour Movement should become revolutionary once more.[13]

IX

THE PARASITISM OF LABOUR

IT is a *national* necessity that the Labour movement should become revolutionary once more. For, when we are congratulating ourselves on our instinctive, and apparently reasonable, certainty that the economic and social revolution of this country will be gradual, what we are really congratulating ourselves upon is the delayed consequences of a monopoly position which itself no longer exists. Hence there is a fundamental unreality in the attitude and policy of Labour to-day. It accepts the old system, and on to the old system seeks to fasten, parasitically, high wages, social services, and unemployment insurance. These parasitic additions, can only be endured by the old system during a period of monopoly, or a period in which the consequences of monopoly endure; the moment – we are living in it now – when these extraordinary conditions have ceased, the parasitic accretions begin to prevent the old system from working at all. The industrial machine begins steadily to run down; it 'slips greasily into decay.' Hence the real truth of the charge brought by the clearer-headed capitalists that our English Socialism is a movement that will neither allow Capitalism to function, nor undertake to function itself. Hence the utterly false position in which Labour was caught at the General Election of October last, when a vote for Labour actually was a vote for uncontrolled national collapse. The issue was between a Capitalism demanding to be allowed to function, and a parasitic Socialism which would choke the Capitalist process while having no purpose or plan of its own with which to replace it. That stupid situation was due to Labour having consented to form a minority Government, a consent which was tantamount to declaring itself in fact completely bourgeois. This basic error was, however, not merely a mistake in tactics made in ignorance; it was the expression of the real temper of the Labour leaders in England. It was revealed to us, and to all the world, by the final outcome. Mr. Macdonald and Mr. Snowden, the two ablest of the Labour leaders, became the acknowledged champions and the actual leaders of the national bourgeoisie.

That was a fantastic situation, from which the bulk of the Labour members revolted upon no conviction whatever, but merely upon instinct. While Mr. Macdonald and Mr. Snowden were logical, consistent, realistic; the decisive portion of the Labour Party, in which the direct influence of the Trade Unions was paramount, did not dare to take responsibility for a cut in unemployment benefit. This was not really cowardice, although Mr. Macdonald and Mr. Snowden were indubitably sincere in denouncing it as cowardice – the conviction of Mr. Snowden's scathing anger, in particular, will not be forgotten by those who listened to him on the wireless – and although the majority of the Labour leaders who went into opposition certainly believed that their own cowardice was real, as it was. It was the influence of what was genuinely Labour in the Labour Party, instinctively refusing to countenance any reduction whatever in the standard of living of the proletariat. It was a spark of the *revolutionary* spirit: *fiat justitia, pereat mundus.*

Fiat justitia, indeed; *pereat mundus* be damned! The conscious proletariat, if it is conscious, will not in itself slide into any such insane conclusion. The policy promulgated by the leaders of the Labour Party in the October election was insane; so insane that it was manifest that no single one of them believed in it. Those who were more clear-headed (Mr. Cole and Mr. Bevin, for example) contented themselves with the enunciation of a programme of aspirations which would, in every respect, have commanded the adherence of Mr. Macdonald himself – the only difference being that Mr. Cole and Mr. Bevin demanded international conferences (to stabilize world-prices and what not) which Mr. Macdonald well knew could never be convoked, because the vital participants (France and America) would refuse to enter. This was not politics even; it was playing at politics.[14] The simple fact of the situation on the Labour side was that its leaders were required to furnish a policy to defend an instinctive reaction – *an instinctive reaction which was not their own.* They were bourgeois politicians, not revolutionary Socialists; if ever they had been revolutionary Socialists, they had forgotten all about it. In the few cases where it had been once an instinct, the experience of prosperity, instead of being used to make themselves *conscious* leaders of the party to which they belonged, had transformed them from proletarians into bourgeois. In the years when they ought to have been acquiring a philosophy, educating themselves for their chosen function, deepening into a basic and ineradicable conviction the instinctive motions of their youth, they allowed themselves to be caught up into the Parliamentary machine and quietly emasculated. Their true function, to educate the solid nucleus of the Labour Movement into consciousness of its real aims, to be *themselves* that consciousness, had been completely neglected. They became parasitic themselves, and suffered the men behind them to become parasitic as well.[15] When the parasitism of the English Labour Party became impossible, when it threatened to bring down the tree to which it clung, there was really only one thing for the Labour leaders to say – the one thing they dared not say, even if they knew it (which they did not) – namely, that they had been leading Labour on a false road for years. They had been lulling themselves, their party and the nation into a sense of false security.

For the truth which the Labour leaders have yet to learn, and which if they will not learn and impart, other leaders must be found to learn and impart, is that *Labour in England must be a party of revolutionary Socialism.* If it does not want to be that then the Labour Party must divide into those who do want to be revolutionary Socialists and those who do not. Those who do not will find their permanent home among the bourgeois parties. And this 'must' in the sentence 'Labour in England *must* be a party of Revolutionary Socialism' – is not merely the 'must' of moral exhortation (though it is that as well), it is the 'must' of economic and social and historic necessity.

The day of parasitic 'socialism' is over. It has reached its apogee of material benefit for the working-classes, and those benefits must now begin to be withdrawn. For they depend on the profitable functioning of the system on which they are parasitic. When that system

F   81

ceases to function profitably, because of its parasitic encumbrances, it ceases to function at all. Capitalistic industrialism must make profits, or cease. The notion that it can still be conducted when profits have ceased is fallacious. That it has taken hold of this country at all is only another consequence of our former position of privilege and monopoly, because of which this country had accumulated vast reserves of wealth (in the shape mainly of overseas investments) which could be used, and have been used, to balance the national account. But the time comes, and has come now, when these reserves are exhausted.[16] At that moment, there is nothing for it but to begin, systematically and steadily, to reduce Labour's share. There is, ultimately, no alternative; because Labour itself, which could enforce the only alternative, has acquiesced in the system of competitive capitalism, and its own parasitism upon it. It has no clear vision of the alternative, still less any effective will towards it. In such a situation it is manifest that the capitalist system must go on its own inevitable way: the share of Labour must go on being reduced.

That is what is bound to happen in the next few years in this country. Temporary mitigations produced by the abandonment of the gold standard, and a mildly hectic revival of our export trade, are in fact quite illusory. In so far as this results in a reduction of *national* standard of living, it presents the appearance of equality of sacrifice. Mathematical equality of sacrifice it certainly is. But we are dealing with human beings, not with mathematical units; and the worker at least knows that ten per cent off an unemployed man's benefit of 25s. a week and ten per cent off, say, my own effective income of £750 a year is not, humanly speaking, equality of sacrifice at all. While my £750 is reduced to an effective £675, his 25s. is reduced to 22s. 6d. It means that I can keep my children fed and clothed and healthy while his are condemned to rickets (for 2s. 6d. a week means the difference between a pint of milk a day and none). And, over and above this so-called 'equality of sacrifice' produced by all devices for temporary mitigation, there is the fundamental fact that a specific effort must be made, not by individuals, but by the capitalist system itself, still further to reduce the share of labour. For the reduction in the share of Labour made by the 'sacrifices all round' consequent on the abandonment of the gold standard, leaves this country in exactly the same position as before relatively to all countries which came off the gold standard. And that is not enough. (Witness our 'permanent' million of unemployed before the world-slump.) We must *improve* our position relatively to that of other countries; that is, we must make in this world where technical achievement is roughly the same – an effort to secure a further reduction in wages. This again will be, in this country, mitigated by an increase in taxation, and an attempt to maintain wages, by means of the social services, at an uneconomic level; but that mitigation again will be only temporary, because the increase of taxation ('burdens upon industry') will compel the still further reduction of wages. We shall be back, essentially, in the system of early capitalism, when parish relief plus economic wages gave the worker a bare level of subsistence.

Against this inevitable depression in its standard of living Labour is bound to react, instinctively. It has known better days, and it knows that even in the best of its better days its share of the national propserity was ridiculously small. Moreover, it will have before its eyes the growing discrepancy between wealth and poverty. For that discrepancy will increase. The lower middle-class bourgeois will be thrust towards the ranks of the proletariat; the distribution of the national wealth will become far less equitable even than it is now, for with the increase of competitive pressure the wealth will be concentrated in fewer and fewer hands. The fantastic comedy of the latest expedient for meeting the national emergency – that the idle rich instead of going to the Riviera should twiddle their thumbs in South Cornwall – will come home to the worker.[17] He will be able to 'prove on his pulses' that he has been hoodwinked by the policy of parasitism.

That moment of inevitable reaction is the moment for which we must prepare. For that will be the decisive moment, if this country is to be spared the horrors of the uncontrolled collapse, which must ensue if Labour is to continue to acquiesce in its role of parasite. It must acquire a consciousness and a will; a consciousness to be aware of the false position into which it has been inveigled by the inducement of immediate material advantages, a will to escape resolutely from that false position. The inducement of immediate material advantages will be no longer on offer; there will be nothing out of which to offer them. On the contrary, the pressure will be constant and constantly increasing to whittle away the material advantages that remain. Then the temptation to take to active resistance will be great indeed. But it will be a temptation essentially of the same order as the temptation to

84

clutch at the immediate material advantages when they were offered. It is a temptation to which it is folly to succumb, except under certain definite conditions. And the first and foremost of these conditions is that Labour should have become conscious of its purposes and its destiny. It must know what it wants. That sounds simple enough. Everybody knows what he wants. That is the grimmest of human fallacies. It takes most men a lifetime to know what they really want, and the vast majority of human beings have not learned it on their death-beds. We all want immediate material advantages – it is the instinct of the human animal within us – but as we slowly approach a condition of fuller awareness, we begin to realize that the clutching at immediate material advantages may result in all advantages being taken from us. The confusion of immediate tangible advantage with ultimate benefit makes fools of us all. By it in the past the Labour Party has been fooled; by it in the present the bourgeoisie of this country is being fooled. Actually, it is to the ultimate advantage of every member of the bourgeoisie in this country that revolutionary Socialism should triumph, for it is the only alternative to national collapse and misery. But things have gone on so long being more or less like what they were before that we cannot believe that things will be really different. We cannot see that economic revolution is bound to come. The water drips on the base of a rock for a thousand years; for a thousand years the peasants who pass it day by day have looked on it as eternal; it was there in the days of their fathers, it will be there in the days of their sons. None the less the rock falls, as like as not on the village which it sheltered. A miracle? No, purely natural; quite inevitable if they had taken the trouble to look.

Thus it is with revolution. Revolution is the moment when quantitative changes, in the great natural process of social life, by mere access of quantity, become qualitative. It takes but one quantitative degree of heat on the thermometer to change water into steam. But the change is a revolution. Two hundred and forty-four degrees through which water can be heated and remain water still; one degree in which it becomes steam. How unreasonable! *Natura non facit saltus.* How *can* Nature disobey its own laws? The answer is that it never does, but it needs eyes that look deep to see the essential continuity of Nature. To shallow-looking eyes, Nature does leap. And it leaps on us – for the leap is revolution.[18]

Labour must cease to be led by shallow-looking eyes. It must cease to confuse immediate benefit with ultimate advantage. That is asking too much of Labour, just as it is asking too much of the bourgeoisie. But the difference between them is that Labour feels the pinch first, and will feel it more and more. Labour will find, and find soon, that by grasping at immediate benefit, it has lost even what it had. Then it will become revolutionary, in instinct, once again, as it was a hundred years ago; then it will be prepared to listen to the men who have told it, day in and day out, that it must be revolutionary, to men who have become revolutionary themselves.

THE MEANING OF REVOLUTION

AH, the word 'revolution.' It would lose all its terrors, if men could understand that revolution is inevitable. But that would mean that they had passed through a revolution in themselves. And that is the crux. If men will not submit to a revolution in themselves they will be forced to undergo a revolution in their outward world. One or the other. If they have not undergone the inward revolution, the outward revolution will come on them like a catastrophe.

The moral of this little book, from this particular angle, is simply that those who have undergone, or can undergo, this revolution in themselves, must become the consciousness of the movement towards revolution that is inevitable in the outward world. It is their duty: they cannot escape it. There is a river to be crossed by us all. We can either strip ourselves naked and take the plunge as conscious men, or be herded into it shrinking and unconscious and be drowned. It sounds rhetorical, and it is metaphorical; but few men realize how *mad* is the world in which we live to-day. We have to resolve to overcome that madness in ourselves. Detachment is not enough. Detachment, unless it passes – as, if it is true detachment, it inevitably will pass – into complete dedication to the cause, the only cause to-day, which will win because it must, and must win because it ought to win – detachment, unless it issues, in pure dedication, is self-corruption, the supreme egoism. What has brought the world of men to this crisis is their individualism. In the old days it mattered little; but to-day, when the body of the world has grown homogeneous, the individualisms of men are become the internecine conflict of the new world-organism. The body of the world has outgrown its consciousness. The body of the world demands health and life and growth, but the minds and hearts of men will not allow it. In such a conflict it is the minds and hearts of men that must be shattered. For consciousness that is not integral to the body in travail will be cast off like a husk at the birth.

If men will not give up their individualisms, then they will be taken from them by force. The body of the world will live, no matter what we do. But if we can sacrifice our individualisms enough to see how the body of the world is striving in a deathly grip with the fetters our individualisms have imposed upon it, then we shall know what we must do. The way is clear. We have only to make the final sacrifice of our individualism, and identify ourselves entirely with that element in the body of the world through which the new life must come.

I repeat my simple figure. Capitalistic industrialism has made the world one body – one giant body, with veins and nerves. There was no way in which this giant body could have been created save by capitalistic industrialism. If we see what might have been done to save the giant body from the disease with which it labours, we see immediately that it could not have been done. It would have required from the human race a level of self-abnegation which is inconceivably remote from it even to-day. The giant body had to be created, and there was but the one way to create it. But because it was created in that way it is now in agony from top to toe. We feel the agony of its unconscious conflict, and we shall feel it more and more. None the less, a mighty and wonderful work has been achieved: the world-body *exists*. It was not; now it is.

But now the individualisms that created it are its disease. They prevent it from growth, they prevent it even from life. The parts will receive, but they will not give. In the great world body it is now dimly felt that its parts must live by one another, or they die; but it is only the dying parts that feel it. The parts which, quite falsely, imagine they flourish because they have accumulated the blood which is the life of all, refuse to believe that the only way to health is sacrifice. Why should they believe it? Since when has this new doctrine been current in the world? The appeal for sacrifice sounds, in the ears of those to whom it is made, like a squeal for pity. And is it really anything else? Since when has pity prevailed between nation and nation? Have *we* been pitiful?[19] Has Germany? But, alas, even if the appeal were heard, it would make no difference. The nations are enemies; inevitably enemies. The world-state of bourgeois idealism is a dream. Because you cannot overcome individualism as between nations until you have overcome individualism within the nations themselves. While capitalistic individualism exists at home, the nation is the potential and indeed the actual enemy of every other nation. Enlarge the bounds of your nation (if you can) to embrace the Empire, and the Empire becomes the unit of economic hostility – more formidable, more to be feared, more to be fought.

Neither in the world of nations, nor in the world of the nation, will individuals sacrifice their interests. They cannot do it. It is impossible. They have not reached that stage of ethical development. But there is a handful of individuals – hundreds, thousands, may be hundreds of thousands who have reached it. They have learned, or begun to conjecture, that the moment is come when they must sacrifice their *all*. At first slowly, then with slowly increasing speed, then in the last hundred years with a truly sickening acceleration, first the nation, then the world of nations has become one *body*. The vast world is one Man. And that one Man is sick, as individual men, time out of mind, have been sick; he is divided within him. There is unconscious growth below, but the mind above is fixed. The pangs of rebirth are at hand. He dreams of better things, he desires better things; but how to achieve them he does not know. The World Man now longs, as the individual man has longed, time after time, for newness of life. And the answer to the World Man is the same answer that was given to individual men two thousand years ago. 'He that loseth his life, the same shall save it.'

Just as through the whole length of the great epoch of which we are the heirs, the religion of disinterestedness has been incessant in its appeal to men since it was first proclaimed, so in the modern world the politics of disinterestedness – Communism – has been incessant in its appeal to men since it was first proclaimed. Jeer at it, sneer at it, persecute it, still it endures, still it grows. For like the religion of which it is the only counterpart in the world of action, it *changes* men. Suddenly, they become from dreamers, men of action;

for suddenly they see that nothing matters but this cause; suddenly, they know that Destiny demands them wholly for its instruments, that by this way, and by no other way, can they annihilate *themselves*, and be. Their faith may seem crude, their dogmas harsh. That is because you do not know, within you, what they mean. The faith of the early Christian was crude, his dogmas harsh; but they were the husk of a seed that created a new world. That new world is now the old one, which is now crumbling before our eyes. But as then, so now, there is a new faith, with new dogmas; and they once more are the husk that contains the seed that will create a new world. That new world, also, will pass: one day it too will become old. There is no finality in Communism, but it is the necessary beginning of a new world-epoch. It is the mode by which the religion of disinterestedness becomes pure action.

To believe in, to pursue, to give oneself to, Communism in this country does not mean to become a 'Communist'; it means to devote oneself to the task of making the Labour Party Marxist and revolutionary once more. The English Communist is the man who works with those and for those who aim at a real social *revolution*, at the complete eradication of the capitalist system. It is the revolution that matters; the name of Communist does not. It seems to me fantastic to suppose that in this country the social revolution should ape the manners of the Russian Revolution; it seems to me natural to suppose that the experience of the next few years will be such as to make Communism appear to a decisive minority of Englishman completely reasonable. In England, too, we can expect to be be allowed to put the Communist case in season and out of season without hindrance. How long that freedom will continue I have no idea. It depends upon how quickly the fundamental Marxist vision permeates the Labour Party, which is its natural instrument. If the Labour Party becomes radically Marxian, instead of parasitic and sentimental, why, then, the cause is as good as won. And the condition of this permeation of the Labour Party is the increase of those intellectuals to whom Communism is veritably the one religious faith. If this book has served to increase their number by a dozen, or even by one, it has not failed.

XI

LABOUR AND LEADERS

Such men, and such alone, are required if the real
work is to be done. For there is one manifest danger,
at which we have already hinted. Marxism is two
things: it is the ethical passion of disinterested action,
and it is the intellectual passion of disinterested seeing;
it is a morality of self-dedication to a revolutionary
cause, and it is a doctrine of historical materialism.
It is not difficult to be Marxist in the second sense,
while carefully refraining from being Marxist in the
first.[20] The history of Continental Marxism is strewn
with comfortable heresies of this kind, which make of
the Marxian doctrine of economic and historical
necessity an ethical justification of the abuses that exist.
But Marxian Communism is a veritable religion – the
absolute antithesis and counterpart to Catholicism.
To accept the Marxian objectivity without the Marxian
ethical passion is a pernicious and detestable heresy,
to be extirpated if it arises in this country, with the
equivalent of fire and sword; to inherit the Marxian
ethical passion without the Marxian objectivity is also
a heresy, though a rarer and a more pardonable one,
but it too must be fought out of existence. At this
moment of the world's history the waste of ethical
passion is not a tragedy but a crime. Marxian Communism is a combination into a perfect dynamic unity of
ethical passion and intellectual objectivity. Hence its
impregnable strength. It is the synthesis after which

the modern mind has groaned and travailed until now. For ethical passion without intellectual objectivity is tragedy; and intellectual objectivity without ethical passion is fatalism. The one is wasted action, the other is no action at all. But Marxian Communism is pure effective action – action completely relevant to the inevitable historical process – action without one drop of waste, without the possibility of tragedy. For if the individual perishes in this cause, he perishes without regret. He has been utterly used for the future. His conscious mind and his instinctive being are at one. He has done what he chose to do, he is what he chose to be. He can never be the unconscious victim; at worst, or at best, the conscious and willing sacrifice.

Thus the conscious Communist is animated and governed by his dedication to destiny. The ways and means of that dedication are the ways and means that are appropriate to this moment in which he lives. To imagine that the ethic of non-resistance is required of the Communist to-day is to fail in that intellectual objectivity which is imagination. Non-resistance to evil was once the order of the day, when there was nothing that could resist it; resistance is the order of to-day when the power that can and must resist is in being, but is merely unconscious of its existence and its strength. For non-resistance to evil was once the perfect and selfless assertion of life, for the reborn individual; to-day the position is wholly changed. The way of perfect and selfless assertion to-day is complete identification with the existing power of resistance to evil, for that identification demands the complete sacrifice of *our* ego. Non-resistance does not.

This is the fallacy that vitiates all modern professions of non-resistance. Men are intuitively aware of the fallacy, but they do not know how to formulate and expose it. The fallacy of non-resistance in the English world is that it is addressed to an ethical consciousness which in practice admits its justification. A world, in which practice admits non-resistance, and either sentimentally acclaims its apostles as martyr-heroes, or good-humouredly accords them the privileges of the second division, is a world in which non-resistance has become ineffective. Objectively, non-resistance is ineffective, because it is allowed; subjectively, it is ineffective because the non-resister knows he is safe. And this knowledge of safety undermines and nullifies the annihilation of the ego which is the living principle of non-resistance. Our modern apostles of non-resistance ascribe the safety which is accorded them to the ethical influence of *their* attitude; it has nothing whatever to do with them. Their safety is due to the ethical influence of the heroes before them – of one hero in particular – for whom non-resistance meant extermination. There was once a world in which non-resistance was positive and dynamic; that world is gone. And in our bones, if not in our minds, we know it. In a world in which there is no resistance to non-resistance, non-resistance is futility.

That does not mean that the duty of resistance, which is consciously upon every conscious Communist and instinctive in the heart of every unconscious one, is to be expressed in truculent processions and sham militarisms. That is *imitation*. And if there is one conviction above all others with which the conscious Communist must be imbued it is that *imitation* is fatal.

No fully conscious Communist *can* imitate any previous manifestation of Communism. There may be resemblances between the manifestations of a conscious English Communism, and the manifestations of Russian Communism; but they will be resemblances only. The moment that deliberate imitation enters in, the true and creative dynamic of Communism has been perverted. Hence, the ineffectiveness of the English 'Communist' party, distinctively so-named. There can be no greater crime against Communism than to be ineffective. For it is essential to true Communism that its action should be shaped by the objective situation. Anything else is play-acting, no matter how sincere and impassioned may be those engaged in it; imitation of Russian methods, which are entirely irrelevant to our English situation, is indeed the strict counterpart to the play-acting of non-resistance in the modern world. Such specious 'resistance' and such specious 'non-resistance' are blood-brothers. That is why they are often found united in the same person.

Communism is pure action; therefore it is wholly effective action. Its resistance must inevitably be shaped in accordance with this inward dynamic. It pursues the maximum of economy in action, in itself as means, and in the world-body as end. Therefore the immediate aim of the conscious Communist is given: it is to make the impulse to resistance, which is the impulse to revolution, conscious in those in whom it is instinctive. Now, it is sheer tomfoolery to imagine that there is in this country any considerable body of workers who have an instinctive impulse towards bloody revolution. They have as a body an instinctive impulse against it. That is why it is not easy to convince them that they have, as they plainly have, and must inevitably have, an instinctive impulse towards revolution itself.

The word sticks in their gizzards. First and foremost then the duty of the conscious Communist, seeking to make the revolutionary impulse conscious in those in whom it is simply an instinct, is to insist upon and to make clear the real meaning of the revolution which must come – to make the true idea of revolution familiar. There is nothing very fearful in the idea: it is nothing more, though nothing less, than a *complete* economic change, the complete extirpation of the system of individualistic capitalism. The conscious Communist must make clear that nothing less than this complete change is of any avail; and that it follows, necessarily, that any line of action taken by the workers which, however rich in specious immediate advantage, renders more difficult that complete economic change, must be inexorably rejected. For Labour to consent, as it has done in the past, to run the government of this country on the old capitalist system is self-stultification of the movement as a whole, and in its leaders culpable ignorance or culpable treachery. If Labour accepts the responsibility of government again in this country, it must be as a majority government, with the definite and avowed programme of the complete abolition of the capitalist system.

But, it will be urged, if Labour openly professes this purpose, it will never win a majority in this country: the free and enlightened electors will never accept such a programme. Now, to *assume* such an absolute and unchanging refusal on a part of the majority of the voters of this country to accept the total abolition of economic individualism is a most dangerous defeatism: it is an unconscious treachery to Labour, and it is also a treachery to the nation. England may be, I believe it is, better at heart than we know. That is not to say that we are entitled to reckon it probable that the programme of economic revolution will win a parliamentary majority in this country. That no man can tell. But one thing is certain: that the only practical, and the only right policy is to put this issue clearly to the test. The nation is sick of politicians who dare not lead, who excuse themselves for their own cowardice by saying that those they represent will not stand the thing of which they themselves are afraid. And anyhow the question is whether a *majority* of voters in this country will accept the revolutionary programme. We have seen that Labour, back on its haunches, can poll one-third of the votes on a false issue. The result of an appeal on the true issue might be startling, above all if the intervening time has been used in honest and devoted propaganda. Further, a vital consideration which this defeatism leaves wholly out of the reckoning, because it has no real convictions, is that the next few years will almost certainly prove to be years of hard practical education in Marxism. If the Marxian diagnosis is correct, then indeed there is a bad time coming.[21] The conscious Communist believes that the Marxian diagnosis is correct; his mind approves it, his instinct endorses it: he reads the signs of the times, and is prepared. The fact that he alone is prepared for what is coming may well be, in itself, decisive. If he now has the courage of his convictions, and proclaims them openly, during the coming period of consolidated bourgeois government, it is quite on the cards – extravagant though it may sound – that Communism, English Communism, humane Communism, may have an actual majority at the next election. And there is this certain fact that unless the Labour opposition is Marxist and revolutionary, it will be nothing. For against the consolidated bourgeois parties there can be no opposition of principle, no real opposition, unless it is revolutionary: anything else *must* be eyewash. The simple facts of the present Parliamentary situation enforce a revolutionary Socialism on the Labour opposition.

Thus we see even in the detail of the present English political situation the necessity of a conscious revolutionary programme for Labour. That is, of course, not a singular and astonishing 'coincidence'; it is the manifest consequence and corollary of the world economic situation. What has happened is simply this: that the realities of the world economic situation, the death agony of individualistic capitalism, has enforced upon the parliamentary parties of this country the pure Marxian cleavage – the bourgeois-'national' on one side, the proletarian-international on the other. That this Marxian cleavage has been produced without the parties themselves being conscious of what was happening is simply the evidence of its crucial significance. It is with nations as with men: it is the things which happen in the unconsciousness of a country which matter. What we have to do is to become conscious of them.

From this angle the actual political situation in England becomes clear. What has happened is that Labour, quite instinctively and unconsciously – quite foolishly indeed from an intellectual-realistic standpoint – has been flinging itself against the world economic situation to which this country, by its precedence and superiority in economic organization, and therefore in organic sensitiveness, is peculiarly responsive. This is a capitalistic country; and *all* its parties, in their calculating consciousness, are capitalistic. Labour, in its consciousness (for, we repeat, its leaders *are* its consciousness) is capitalistic; to be parasitic on capitalism is to be capitalistic. The mentality by which it has been led may be judged by the sapient pronouncement of the Rt. Hon. Herbert Morrison, after the deluge. 'If capitalism could stand all the social expenditure which ideally we desire, capitalism would be a good system.' (*The Week End Review*, Nov. 7th, 1931.) That is a morally rotten notion. If capitalism could stand all the social expenditure which the Right Honourable Herbert 'ideally desires' – in contrast, I suppose, to really desiring it – still it would be a *rotten* system – morally debilitating to the workers on the one hand and to the capitalists on the other. But to the workers above all, for it offers them simply an eternity of parasitism – one everlasting *panem et circenses*. And that policy of moral debilitation proceeds from a defeatist mentality. The Right Honourable Herbert Morrison may be a sincere and admirable man, for aught I know; but as a Labour leader, he has the elements to learn.

In its consciousness, which is its leaders, Labour is capitalistic. Therefore when the decisive issue arose, when the contradiction of the world-economic situation was thudding in distracted pulse-beats on England which is still the heart of the economic world-body, the clear-thinking elements of the Labour consciousness went over to the bourgeoisie. The decisive issue simply revealed them as what they had always been – bourgeois Radicals. Perhaps one or two equally sincere elements of the same consciousness – the unconscious elements of it, not the conscious ones – went the other way on sheer instinct. But the great bulk of them simply fled: because they had not annihilated themselves, they were morally annihilated. There was only one case to be made for Labour, and they dared not make it: for it was not an intellectual case at all – intellectually, Labour had no case – but an instinctive and religious one. The only case was to declare openly that though the bourgeois, the 'nation,' perish, yet Labour must live: the mind may perish, but the body must live. And the declaration of this case inevitably involved an open profession of revolution. Therefore the Labour leaders dared not make it, because they have never dared to believe it. Therefore, having no belief, they had no case. For, we repeat, intellectually there was no meeting the challenge of Mr. Macdonald and Mr. Snowden, who had the courage of their convictions, which were the same as the convictions of the demoralized Labour leaders. And morally there was no meeting that challenge. Between men of the same fundamental convictions the moral superiority of the man who declares them over the man who is afraid to is overwhelming. There was a bad smell about the Labour leaders and their vamped-up programme of infinite parasitism, and they paid the penalty. For there was nothing for it for the *conscious* revolutionary but to vote bourgeois. It is no use voting for deliquescence and decay.

Labour had to remain in being, but Labour had to

be defeated as it had deserved – heavily. A time of purgation and of purging was necessary for the English Labour Party. There had to be a definite break with the tradition of parasitism. The conditions for that break are now in being. There is the bourgeois-national block on one side – the proletarian-international nucleus on the other – and the bourgeois-national leaders of the proletarian-international nucleus are where they ought to be – chiefly on the scrap-heap. There they can meditate – this book.

They will, if they read it, bring out the old weary defeatist arguments – that Labour will never win on an open programme of economic revolution. To hell with these arguments! The business of Labour is to save its soul from those who would corrupt it. It is not winning that matters, it is saving one's soul alive; for the Labour party, if it saves its soul alive, is bound to win – and to win handsomely, and outright and soon. To put winning first is to condemn Labour to ultimate defeat and this nation to the horrors of slow collapse. Not merely in actual political practice, for the able heads of the bourgeois-national bloc will tear to shreds all the futile argument for further parasitism, and Labour will become a thing of contempt; but by moral necessity also, for the conscious revolutionary cannot put winning first. It is a moral impossibility. It is the old, old story, couched in modern terms: 'Seek ye first the Kingdom of Heaven and all these things shall be added unto you.'

Therefore, if the discredited leaders of Labour now bring forth the argument that Labour cannot win on an avowed revolutionary programme, this is what we shall say to them: By that argument you are finally revealed as unworthy to lead Labour any more. For Labour *is* revolutionary, and it cannot win except as revolutionary. If it wins as anything else, it loses. 'What shall it profit a man if he gain the whole world and lose his own soul?' The texts keep cropping up – not coincidentally, not from any unconscious urge towards religious gerrymandering on my part, but simply because they are the adequate, and the only adequate comments on a situation which really is this: Shall we, or shall we not, make completely effective the ethical passion of Jesus in an objective situation – the first in history – which demands it? Now is the crucial moment. Never in the whole world history till now has there been a chance to do it. And now that chance is a necessity. No wonder the texts conspire.

The only worthy, the only effective leaders of Labour now, are those who are resolved that Labour shall never lose its soul again, even though the whole would be offered it. 'If capitalism could stand all the social expenditure which ideally we desire, capitalism would be a good system' – such and similar are the words in which the whole world is offered to Labour; if they are listened to the soul of Labour is lost. Aye, and the whole world too. For it is not the future of Labour that depends on Labour, but the future of the world. Who cares a rap for the future of Labour as such? No true Labour man. He knows, if his opponents do not, that what he fights for in Labour is the universal manhood of human beings. It is against the degradation of that manhood that he fights instinctively, and he will fight till he drops. He alone fights *for* his enemies, at the moment that he fights against them. They fight only for themselves – for the mortal and perishable thing. He fights for that which is immortal and imperishable in them – the Universal Man that will not and must not be degraded.

XII

THE IMMEDIATE TASK

THE one thing needful in these coming years is that Labour should become openly and avowedly revolutionary, in the fundamental sense we have described. It is the only possible policy now, if Labour is to have a policy at all; it is the only right policy, and it is the only policy that will succeed.

But what do we mean by 'success'? Suppose, in the best case, that Labour, openly avowing its intention of eradicating capitalism, were to win a parliamentary majority. It sounds optimistic, we admit; but it is far less optimistic than it sounds. We must remember, all the time, that the chances are heavy, the odds even overwhelming, that the condition of the capitalist world-organism will go from bad to worse with sickening speed in the next four or five years. Every attempt at palliation will come too late; because at every level, international and national, even the temporary remedy required will be too radical to be applied. A few years more slowing down of the English industrial machine, and heaven alone knows how chastened the bourgeois will be. If Labour has pursued the only sane, the only real, and the only right policy, it will be the only party with an alternative to the proven bourgeois-national futility. The electorate will turn to it in sheer desperation. After all, revolutionary Labour will be *the* Opposition and there will be no choice, politically. And, in reality, there will be none. For, if

Labour shilly-shallies, and again turns bourgeois-radical, it can offer only a repetition of what has happened already.

Revolutionary Labour, then, we suppose, has won a parliamentary majority. What then? Can we suppose that, simply because there is a revolutionary majority over the bourgeois in Parliament, that capitalism – economic individualism – will capitulate? Take the case of Germany and Austria, some months further along the road to economic disintegration than we. What has happened there is the formation of a militant 'national' party, on the Fascist model. Will not the same happen here? [22]

Indubitably there lies the danger. It seems to me possible and even probable that in this country revolutionary Socialism may get to the point of a parliamentary majority, in spite of the overwhelming odds. But I cannot feel certain that capitalism would capitulate. I know how terribly hard it has been for me, personally, to accept the Communist ideal – how much I have had to surrender, how stubborn the resistance within me to the sacrifice it requires. I cannot but believe that this stubborn resistance in the individual will have its counterpart in a stubborn resistance in the nation. It is the same resistance writ large.

And yet, and yet – it may be my naive English idealism, my ineradicable faith in the instinctive wisdom, the long and unique political experience of this country – I cannot believe it will come to that. Russian Marxism, I know, is inexorable on the point. Capitalism will never capitulate. It will fight to the last ditch, and it must be extirpated there. And, of course, there is the Russian example.

One thing is certain: Russia is not England, and it is manifest madness to assume, or even to imagine, that revolution in England will follow the Russian pattern. *To create in this country a 'revolutionary situation' such as existed in Russia in 1917 would require that the complete economic collapse against which conscious Communism is our one real safeguard should actually have occurred.* If England gets to the condition of Russia in 1917, the condition posited as necessary by all the Communist theorizing based on the Russian example, then we might as well march voluntarily into the lethal chamber. Our failure, our national degradation, will be so ignominious that we had better disappear from the face of the earth. The condition of Russia in 1917 was not appalling for Russia, nor was it unthinkable by a Russian; but that such a condition should come to pass in England would be in itself the final and damning proof that this nation had no part to play in the future of the world. For an Englishman, however objective, however dispassionate, however complete in his acceptance of the fundamental Marxian positions, it is *unthinkable* that England should ever decline into the condition of Russia in 1917. *In other words, the fundamental postulate of all Communism that bases itself on the Russian pattern is objectively false.*

Hence, we arrive once more, and by a different road, at the necessity of an *English* Communism. We shall be excommunicated by the Third International, of which one fundamental dogma is that there can be no national Communism. That is manifestly the height of stupidity: for nothing could well be more national than Russian Communism. It is, indeed, high time that a few English Communists gave a piece of their mind to the sea-green incorruptibles of Moscow. They are devoted men and we respect them, even for their national idiosyncrasy. But that they should not respect our idiosyncrasy, but rather forbid it us, is quite intolerable. And it is abysmally stupid. We must cut ourselves adrift from Moscow until Moscow has become Marxian enough to admit the objective situation of England – a country which, when all the worst is said, has not done so badly by the world in the matter of political example. Moscow has required us to swallow its dogmas – dogmas not of Marxism, but of Russia; we will retort by requiring Moscow to swallow one of ours, namely, *that every country gets the Communism it has deserved.*

Here then is the first function of English Communists – to give the movement in England a specifically English intelligence. That alone will require all the powers of intellectual ability and ethical devotion we are likely to enlist in the cause. Yet this is supremely necessary. For nothing hinders, and nothing will hinder, the progress of true Communism in this country so much as the conviction that Communism is not native to us. Communism is native to every capitalist country; it is more native to England than to any other country in the world, first, because we are the oldest capitalist country in the world, and, second, because we have learned by experience how to give some political expression to our ethical passion. Communism is infinitely more native to England than to Russia. What, on the other hand, is infinitely more native to Russia than to England is terrorism and bloody revolution.[23] We English Communists will, at any rate, be objective enough not to treat Communism and bloody revolution as identical.

We must do it as honourable men; we must do it as clear-seeing men. To pretend that there is any widespread feeling of class-*hatred* against the English bourgeoisie is ridiculous; to pretend to oneself that there is any probability of stimulating such a feeling of class-hatred is to indulge in evil dreams. Class-warfare and class-hatred are utterly different things. Class-warfare exists; it is a fundamental reality. It exists in the unconsciousness of English Labour. Our duty, as true Communists, is to bring the reality of class-warfare from the unconsciousness into the consciousness of the English proletariat, *and by so doing to prevent the class-warfare from becoming class-hatred*. That degeneration of class-warfare into class-hatred is not inevitable. The English bourgeoisie is often stupid, but it has a tradition and a record of devoted service which can be paralleled in the bourgeoisie of no other nation on earth. To compare an English civil servant with a Russian official, to compare even an English parson with an orthodox priest of the old regime is scarcely even possible, so wide asunder are the terms to be compared. Against such men it is impossible to engineer class-*hatred*. It would be practical folly and moral perversity to attempt it. Only if, under the 'menace' of Communism, the character of the English bourgeoisie degenerates completely, will class-hatred become a reality in England.

The objector will say: 'But your policy and programme is to make the "menace" of Communism real. Under pressure of the menace which you would make open and avowed, the character of the English bourgeoisie will degenerate – and you will be confronted by armed resistance: an English Nazi movement.' Well, it may be so; but equally it may not be so. The English Communist must, in his mind and soul, be prepared for either alternative. He must be prepared ultimately to resist armed attack by arms. But that is a second best. His primary aim must be to carry through the economic revolution by peaceful and legal means. And that is not a fantastic and 'idealistic' aim. It is the necessary first step in a purely realistic policy of Communism in this country. That is, or should be, obvious to an English Communist. For his first task on any showing is to bring over a section of the English bourgeoisie to the side of Communism, in order to make Communism a *conscious* movement in this country. It has to become a movement with impregnable, philosophical and religious convictions of its own; to reveal itself as what it is: the one truly coherent world-view available to the modern man. Englishmen have to learn to be *proud* to be Communists, because they know they are the only conscious inheritors not merely of the political and economic experience of this country, but of Christian civilization as a whole. They, and they alone, are completely surrendered to be the conscious vehicles of the organic sequence of history. Intellectually, spiritually, ethically, the choice before the conscious Englishman to-day is to be a Communist or *nothing*. His nothingness may take the most diverse forms; æsthetic dilettantism, snobbish economic sapience, superficial 'action,' pessimistic neo-Catholicism. But each and all alike are forms of nothingness: manifestations of non-belief. Ultimately, a man has to believe. At a crucial moment of the world's history he must believe, or perish. There is now, and always has been, only one way of achieving a belief – through the final sacrifice of the ego. To-day, there is only one way of sacrificing the ego. No form of 'religion' can offer it. For all forms of 'religion' to-day have as their practical principle the preservation of the ego, masquerading as the 'values of the past.' To-day, as in crucial moments before to-day, there is one way and one way alone towards the complete sacrifice of the ego. To-day it is Communism. Therefore Communism is the enemy of all 'religions,' because it is itself the one religion.

And, I believe, in his unconsciousness, the bourgeois of to-day knows this. He is doubtful, bewildered, afraid; obscurely, yet vitally, he is aware that he does not *believe* even in his own position of privilege. As for religious belief, he has none. And those two central unfaiths of the modern bourgeois are implicit in one another. He does not believe in himself, therefore he cannot believe in God. 'Why should he believe in God?' comes the snigger of the futile intelligentsia. Simply because to carry the life of the world through crisis, a man must believe in God. 'But the Communist himself does not believe in God!' Oh, you *fools*! What difference is there between believing in God and believing in Man – in life, in the future, in the unknown. The Communist does not believe in past Gods, he rejects them utterly and for ever, because he believes in the God that creates himself eternally in the everlasting body of Man. It is because we do not know what *belief* is any more that we cannot see the simple fact staring us in the face that Communism is the one living religion in the Western world to-day.

Because it is the one possible, the one inevitable creed for conscious men. It is the men who have pushed their consciousness to the extreme, without faltering or falling, who, if they have stumbled in the road to consciousness have picked themselves up and struggled on, who have not been able to flinch from the destiny that was upon them – to question everything, to question the inmost reality of themselves – it is these men who come at the last, as to an inevitable goal, to the knowledge of the religion of Communism. They know the blessedness of final and irrevocable self-surrender.

And it is to these and such as these that Communism makes its direct and certain appeal, and will make it more and more. There will be more and more Englishmen *proud* to be Communists; who will know in themselves by what impulse Karl Marx was moved when he wrote at the end of the First Manifesto of the Communist Party: 'Communists *scorn* to hide their views and aims.' The pride and scorn of the Communist is the pride and scorn of complete humility. He is impersonally proud: proud that he is being *used*, proud that his destiny is it be used to the uttermost, to be used up and cast aside – proud that he had been found not unworthy to be consumed.

XIII

THE RELIGION OF COMMUNISM

THERE is a mighty force in Communism. It is the focusing into one impersonal point of pure action of ethical disinterestedness and intellectual objectivity. The ethical passion of Communism is not possible without the intellectual disinterestedness; the intellectual disinterestedness is not possible without the ethical passion.[24] It is for the individual who experiences it a dynamic unification. Heart and mind are at one, and pure and necessary action flow out of the unity. It cannot be but that those individuals who have become new men by their experience of Communism should not work a change in the weary intellectual bourgeoisie of to-day. For, after all, what of their doubts have *we* not known? Which of their struggles have *we* not endured? What has been their scepticism compared to ours? We know, of a certainty, that there is not one of their arguments that we cannot annihilate. They have nothing in their armoury for which we are not prepared. Put us to the test, on any ground, and we shall meet it and shall win.

We mystics, we fanatics! Yes, that is true. But we the open-eyed investigators of the things that are. Our strength is not in our mysticism and our fanaticism: it is in our lucidity. We look upon the great world, we look upon ourselves, with serene impartiality. We have no illusions. And out of our serene impartiality, out of our final loss of all illusion, arises mysticism, arises fanaticism. By the depth of their disillusion, cowards are made strong. They have the strength to know themselves for cowards, and be brave: a strength that is not theirs.

It is a portent. Says Mr. Keynes:

'Marxian Socialism must always remain a portent to the historian of opinion – how a doctrine so illogical and so dull can have exercised so powerful and enduring an influence over the minds of men and, through them, the events of history.' (*The End of Laissez-Faire*, *p.* 34.)

Communism is a mighty force, as those who have experienced it know well. It is, to Mr. Keynes, 'illogical and dull.' I suppose he would say the same of the Sermon on the Mount, in his quality of 'historian of opinion.' But what kind of a historian of opinion can he be who blandly assumes that only logical and amusing (the Bloomsbury opposite of 'dull') doctrines have powerful and enduring influence over the minds – shall we not also say the 'hearts' – of men? How, if he did not assume this airy nonsense, should the influence of Communism be a *portent* to him?

To Mr. Keynes, Marxian Socialism is merely 'an example of poor thinking, of inability to analyse a process and follow it out to its conclusion.' It is what always happens: Mr. Keynes has no room for Communism; but Communism has for Mr. Keynes.[24] The intelligence that can really gull itself into believing that 'an example of poor thinking' can change cowards into men has ceased to be an intelligence. Beneath every seeming fanaticism that has changed the world there has been a dynamic reality which, precisely because it is dynamic, cannot be *thought*. If it could be thought, it could not be dynamic. Therefore no economics, not even the Marxian, is a system of thought true to human life. Ultimately, there is no such thing as the economic unit which economics must posit; ultimately there is only the human being. And him you cannot think; him you can only imagine, aye, and love. Marxism is the economics of imagination, which is love.

For the secret of Marx's economics is his immediate vision of the world as the unconscious struggle of humanity towards a better future. Marx saw the body of Western humanity as one body, the body of a Man divided against himself – the rich against the poor, the possessing against the dispossessed. He saw that revolution was inevitable. But why was revolution inevitable? Not because of any mathematical progression of economic units, not because of any abstract economic probability, but because human beings would not suffer the degradation of the divine humanity in themselves. When oppressed humanity *could* stand erect, then it would stand erect, even though the wide arches of the ranged Empire fell. What Marx saw was that the moment was approaching when oppressed humanity could stand erect. That is not economics, it is vision; not theory, but truth.

And Marx put a vision before men's eyes once more. And those who saw it knew that the call was upon them. They must shatter the laws of economics, by performing the simple miracle that blows the laws of economics sky-high. There is no room for Marx in Marxism. There is no room for the disinterested man in economics. He does not exist. He *is* an unimaginable portent. One – two – a hundred – a thousand – ten thousand – disinterested men: men dedicated, men surrendered, men with the last dross of self burnt out of them, and the laws of economics begin to crack into fragments.

There's the paradox; there's the portent, which Mr. Keynes can never understand. How could he? Communism is the economics of disinterestedness. And there can be no such economics. It is the animal that ought not to exist. And yet, it does exist. And why does it exist? Because Marx was a completely disinterested man. There is always hell to pay when a disinterested man gets loose in the world, for he in obedience to the pure disinterestedness that devours him goes on and on. He does not fling himself about. He bides his time, and waits his moment. The interested man is always making his moment; only the disinterested man can afford to wait for his. It is not he who moves. He *is* moved. And the world begins to move with his motion, for he is moving with the motion of the world.

What has made Marxian economics the prodigious force it is? The dynamic of disinterestedness; not the dynamic of interest. That is there, but it is dumb and blind. Something must happen to make that dumb, blind force of the proletariat conscious, aware, convinced. And the happening that is required is the passing over, the dedication, body and soul, to the proletariat of men who do not belong to it. It is not the world process that makes revolution inevitable, it is the moral revolution in the few. The moral revolution of those few also belongs to the world process; and they know it. It is the act of men who see whither the world-process is going, who know why it is going there, who know that there is a choice between catastrophe and control, and that only the complete surrender of themselves can turn it from the worse to the better thing. For revolution can be a thing that comes on the world as hideous disaster, or as a foreknown, controlled change. Marx saw catastrophe impending; he gave his life to make it into conscious change.

The better thing would come; the better thing must come. That Marx saw. But through what horrors and tribulation it would come, if men did not give up their lives to it beforehand! That also Marx saw. Men forget the horrors of world-change; they forget with what travail the new births of the Western world have come; why, they even forget the Great War itself! But Marx remembered these things. He was a man of imagination. And he was more: he was a man of ethical passion. He knew clearly, what we all knew obscurely, that, finally, human destiny *is* in human hands; that, finally, the summons is upon the individual man. He called to men, like the great prophet before him, 'Repent ye, for the kingdom of God is at hand!' Was the coming Reign of God, which Jesus foresaw, a thing of terror or a thing of joy? Scholars do not know. They seldom do know these things, for if they knew, they would cease to be scholars. It was both, as Communism, its earthly paradigm, is both. That the individual man should make the thing of terror a thing of joy, by anticipating the revolution in his own heart and mind, was the whole gospel of Jesus. It is the whole gospel of Marx.

The Communist Manifesto of Marx is the summons to the modern world to repent. It is not easy to repent. It never was. And Christianity has forgotten all it ever knew about repentance. It is devilishly easy to 'be truly sorry.' We are all truly sorry. The economist is truly sorry. But repentance – that is a different kettle of fish. Repentance – *metanoein* – to have one's mind turned upside down. We begin to learn what repentance is when we collide with Communism. Then we are up against the grim reality of repentance. 'What! give up everything?' Yes, give up everything. 'All I possess?' Yes, all you possess. 'But my freedom – surely not that?' Yes, your freedom – that above all else. 'But how can I surrender my freedom: I *am* free?' No. You are not free. Your freedom is bondage – to the desire to do what *you* will; you are the slave of interest and self. Freedom is to be free for ever from that bondage, that slavery. That freedom you will gain; that other 'freedom' – that bondage to the self – Communism will take away. 'But this demand is fearful. Such a thing has never been asked of human men before.' Yes, it has been asked. God and Jesus once demanded it; now it is Man who demands. 'But you want me to destroy myself.' That is required. That you should annihilate your self. Destroy your self, or be destroyed! Choose!

This is the *reality* of repentance. No wonder men begin to fly from it, to the Church, where only the semblance of that sacrifice is now required of them, where they can go through a pantomime of repentence, and retain all they have and are. 'Verily I say unto you, it is easier for a camel to go through the eye of a needle, than for a rich man to enter the kingdom of God.'

Communism demands all we have, and all we are. And because it dares to demand this, it is invincible.

For what is the matter with us, as individuals, to-day is simply this: that no one dares to demand sacrifice enough from us. We are capable of sacrifice. I believe in my heart that England is capable of such sacrifice as the world has never known in a nation. But no one dares to demand it. Yet deep in our hearts we know that this is what we hunger for – to have sacrificed our all, and to be new; to have sacrificed our freedom, and be *free*.

XIV

THE PRACTICAL PROGRAMME

WHAT is the practical programme of Communism – the revolutionary programme, as we have called it – in this country to-day? In reality it is precisely the same as it was in the Communist Manifesto of 1848. But at the present moment it narrows down to one absolutely simple and absolutely decisive issue, upon which there can be no compromise whatever. Any compromise of any kind on this issue is treachery.

There must be a guaranteed decent minimum wage for every man, whether in or out of employment, and this guaranteed decent minimum wage must be established IMMEDIATELY.

That is the one vital issue. Everything else flows necessarily from it. And by this decent minimum wage we mean not the restoration of the ten per cent cut in unemployment benefit, but an increase of at least ten per cent on the uncut figure.

The reply is: 'The country *cannot* pay it.' That is a lie. The country can pay it. But it cannot pay it unless the relatively rich (you and me included) are compelled to make drastic sacrifices.

Labour must be honest, with itself and with the country. It must say outright: 'We demand these sacrifices from you. Will you make them, or will you not?' It must not, for one moment, suffer itself to be led into the mazes of the 'economists.' There Labour will be ambushed and betrayed, every time, and by the 'economists' of Labour worst of all. Remember

Marx's warning: 'Beware of the economists!' They are your servants; do not let them become your masters. It would have been better for the Labour Party if the London School of Economics had never been born.

The true, right and just programme of revolutionary Labour is the simple one we have put forward. It has economic consequences. Those need to be studied, and accepted; to be accepted and proclaimed. Those consequences are revolutionary. Of course. Who expected them to be anything else? But the last thing you will get from economists as a class is revolutionary economics. There has been only one revolutionary economist, and he was Marx. And because he was revolutionary, the economists will not have him. Not because he was a bad economist, but because he was a revolutionary one.

The immediate programme of revolutionary Labour has, necessarily, revolutionary economic consequences. The Labour leaders in the past have always shirked them. Consider the precious London Transport Bill of Mr. Herbert Morrison: the extremest American big business man, plundering the public through a Public Utility Corporation, could desire nothing better than Mr. Morrison has given to Lord Ashfield. Such a man is constitutionally incapable even of imagining, much less of enforcing, the economic consequences of the simple Labour demand. They are these.

To provide the decent minimum wage, credit must be issued by the banks. In order to compel the banks to do this, they must be nationalized, which means they must be put under direct political control. In order that the credit they issue shall be real, and not mere inflation, the issue of credit must be accompanied by taxation so drastic that all incomes would be reduced to a maximum, say, of £1000 a year. Direct taxation is the best means, because it keeps the issue obvious.

This drastic increase of direct taxation must be enacted simultaneously with the establishment of the minimum wage. In other words the Budget must be balanced immediately. Without that inflation will begin, and the minimum wage will be fictitious. With it the minimum wage will be real.

Immediately, with this enormous transfer of purchasing power from the richer to the poorer classes, the wheels of industry will begin to move. Immediately more credit based on the increased supply of real goods will be made available.

Without this transfer of *real* purchasing power, without the practical measure of expropriation on which it must be based, all schemes of amelioration merely by expanding credit are pure inflation.

There is, no doubt, a real danger of sabotage by the interests affected; how real it is, time will tell. But if the clear moral issue is kept before the country, I believe the opposition will crumble by its own inward rottenness. The vital issue, I repeat, is not economic, but *moral*. Economics will adapt themselves to a moral decision. But we must keep the issue clear.

There is no need in this country to proceed to specific acts of expropriation – for example, of the land. That is necessarily involved in the drastic increase of taxation. Nor need we worry about abolishing, or vitally diminishing, the National Debt: that also is involved, practically.

The practical policy of English Communism is

therefore extremely simple. It amounts simply to *the establishment of the decent minimum wage, to all men whether in or out of work, together with the immediate balancing of the Budget by an increase of direct taxation.* No compromise of any sort or kind can be entertained on these essentials.

Educational equality, and the virtual abolition of inheritance, will be found to flow immediately out of this programme. Its economic consequences to our export trade will not be in the least disastrous. That they will *appear* disastrous to 'economists' – even to Labour 'economists' – who cannot free their minds from the unconscious assumptions of economic individualism, is perfectly true. But the mind that cannot free itself from these assumptions is a mind from which we have nothing to expect, and ultimately, nothing to fear.

NOTES

NOTES

[1] 'Surely, at such a moment, the voice ought to be heard of a man whose whole theory is the result of a life-long study of the economic history and condition of England, and whom that study led to the conclusion that, at least in Europe, *England is the only country where the inevitable social revolution might be effected entirely by peaceful and legal means.* He certainly never forgot to add that he hardly expected the English ruling classes to submit, without a "pro-slavery rebellion," to this peaceful and legal revolution.' Engels: Preface to the English Translation of *Das Kapital*.

[2] Actually, the tragedy of Jesus arose directly from the incompatibility of his ethical passion with his environment: the established theocracy of Judaism. Since his ethical passion was himself, i.e. he was totally surrendered to it, he had to pursue his path. Once he saw, quite clearly, that he could not make men understand his gospel, he prepared himself for the final sacrifice, which was inevitable. That he saw it was inevitable, and yet endured it to the end, was his supreme victory. See my *Life of Jesus*; and, for a statement of his story in the terms of a *complete* materialism, *God: An Introduction to the Science of Metabiology.* The title of this book has, I fear, been an impediment to many. But unless the history of Jesus is understood, the history of Marx and Marxism is really unintelligible. The reading of Feuerbach's 'Essence of Christianity' was crucial in the development of both Marx and Engels.

[3]   A poignant example of such a tragedy in modern times was D. H. Lawrence. For an account of it, see *Son of Woman.*

[4]   Marx pointed out how profoundly revolutionary our political evolution had been: it had passed from expropriation to expropriation (e.g. of Church lands in the Reformation, of common lands in the eighteenth century).

[5]   A remarkable example of the combination has appeared in the first number of *Action,* the organ of Sir Oswald Mosley's new Party. It should be kept, by those who are sensitive to the signs of the times, as a perpetual reminder of the condition to which a large and influential section of the English intelligentsia had sunk in the autumn of 1931.

[6]   The church, as institution, has always denied that the Kingdom of God was a condition attainable in this life in spite of the fact that the teaching of Jesus makes nonsense if it isn't. By making the Kingdom of God, first into the Kingdom of Heaven (not an authentic phrase of Jesus at all), and then Heaven after death, the Church neatly deprived the revolutionary doctrine 'it is easier for a camel . . .' of its revolutionary sting. It was castrated. For obviously, no man is rich when he is dead. A living dog is richer than a dead lion. But the Church settled any lingering doubts that even the rich man might have about this method of interpretation: which makes nonsense of the saying, and absurdity of the incident: (For why did the rich young man go sorrowful away? He should have been

most happy). It declared that nothing was easier than for the rich man to enter the Kingdom of God, providing he left some of his property to the Church at death, after enjoying it all his life.

By putting it in this fashion, for clarity's sake, it may seem that I accuse the Church of deliberate hypocrisy. I don't; nor do I accuse parsons to-day of deliberate hypocrisy. The Church has been a struggling animal like everything else. It couldn't preach revolution when the world was not ready for it. And, conversely, because the world was not ready for it, the Church could not see that the essential doctrine of Jesus was revolutionary.

[7] An account of this process – implicit in the still current religious axiom that 'the voice of conscience is the voice of God' – is contained in my book *God*. See also my essay 'The Creation of Conscience' in *The Adelphi* (1929).

[8] Witness the pathetic, but well-intentioned struggle of the late medieval Church against usury: i.e. against 'interest' – the vital, but now decaying, nerve of the modern social organism.

[9] There are some impressive examples of Quaker morality *in act* in the notes to Marx's *Das Kapital*.

[10] True, they were not fully *conscious* human beings. And in these terms Communism is the politics of the fully conscious human being. So it might be defined. In these terms also the immediate practical task of Communism is to bring men into a condition of full consciousness.

I

[11]   This reaction is peculiarly striking in the last writings of D. H. Lawrence. It is the outward indication of his inward failure. Nothing less than radical Communism could have brought peace to his unquiet heart. But he could not accept his rightful destiny of self-annihilation. Therefore his significance, which is great, is purely negative. His novel *Kangaroo* is one of the most profound political treatises of modern times, for it shows the complete moral demand of conscious politics upon the modern man. That Lawrence refused it – 'his great refusal' – does not alter the fact that he was the first modern Englishman to *feel* the sternness of the complete demand.

[12]   Remember the simple judgment passed on Mr. H. G. Wells by Lenin, when they met. 'Heavens! *what* a bourgeois!' Lenin, in the social sense, was every bit as much a bourgeois as Mr. Wells: rather more so. But Lenin knew what the sacrifice of the *ego* meant. Every one outside the ranks of the actual proletariat is a bourgeois unless he has made that sacrifice.

[13]   That this is no idle paradox may be seen by a consideration of Soviet Russia, where it is evident that the proletarian revolution has been the means of keeping Russia in being as a *nation*.

[14]   This is not intended to be a personal criticism of Mr. Cole, whom I honour as one of the most selfless leaders of Labour. But the fact is that he also has allowed himself to be driven into a false position, from which he can now extricate himself only by a sort of disingenuousness. Thus in his recent pamphlet of

dialogues, *The National Government and Inflation*, he makes it appear that the programme of the Labour Party at the election was something quite different from the programme actually proclaimed.

   Q. But the Labour Party insists on balancing the Budget just as much as the National Government.

   A. They say so; but how can they, if they won't cut down the dole?

   Q. Can't they get the money by taxation, and by suspending the Sinking Fund, and economizing on armaments?

   A. Everybody is taxed too much already. At least the richer people are. Taxation kills enterprise.

   Q. So apparently, does economy – of the sort proposed by the National Government. But suppose we taxed the *rentiers*. (p. 8.)

Now this, very plainly, suggests that an increase of direct taxation was part of the Labour Programme at the election. *It was not.* Again,

   X. How could they have balanced the Budget, without cutting the dole?

   Y. In lots of ways. The Trades Union Congress proposed a levy on all incomes to find the money for the unemployed. (p. 15.)

This, again very plainly, suggests that this proposal was part of the Labour Programme at the election. *It was not.*

The Labour Party had not the courage to put such proposals forward. It is not merely an intellectual, but a *moral* mistake to try to make it appear that they did put them forward.

[15] I should perhaps say that I use the term 'parasitic' in a purely scientific sense, to show the nature of the objective situation. I am not using it as a term of vituperation. The Labour movement in this country has been misled through ignorance, and unconsciousness of itself; but the temptation to remain in ignorance and unconsciousness has been uncommonly strong. English prosperity and English political reasonableness together made England singularly recalcitrant to Marxism. The true opportunity is coming now.

[16] I speak in general terms of the realities of the situation. It is open to anyone to say that in fact our reserves in overseas investments are still considerable. But (1) they are now largely unproductive and (2) they are 'frozen.' And the chief reason why they are unproductive and 'frozen' is the running down of *our* national economy. To make our reserves of wealth liquid and fertile, we have to produce more wealth as a national economy in order to send it abroad. As our national economy fails to produce wealth, our *reserves* of wealth also disappear. This may seem a fantastic paradox: but unfortunately it is true. And after all it is only one of the more striking manifestations of the paradox of capitalism.

[17] They have thought better of this.

Sir,—There must be many people among your readers who, while sincerely anxious at the present time to show their patriotic feeling by refraining from spending money in foreign countries, are yet reluctant through reasons of health to run the risk of the uncertainties of an English winter, in however sheltered a

spot. It is in their interest that I venture to trespass on your space in order to bring to their notice once more the great charms of the West Indies as a winter resort.'
> A letter to *The Times*, Nov. 9th, 1931.
Why not try the charms of the Rhondda Valley in winter – a truly sheltered spot? And, why not for variety try it on the dole?

[18] 'What are we to think of a law that asserts itself only by periodical revolutions? It is nothing but a law of Nature, resting on the unconsciousness of the persons concerned.' Engels, quoted by Marx: *Capital*, vol. 1, p. 49.

[19] I should like to register a protest against the complacent smugness of the argument familiar lately in the British Press, that Great Britain worked the gold-standard *altruistically*. Great Britain lent money where it would make a profit and be reasonably secure, in the good old mercantile tradition. To suggest that, following our magnanimous example, France and America should lend money where it is not reasonably secure, is the height of Pecksniffery. The tragedy of our situation is that we are the heart of the world-body. We now feel the necessity of an altruism which we never practised. The necessity is real enough. But how can *we* preach it? The answer is: we shall not be listened to until we have changed.

[20] 'The highest point that can be reached by contemplative Materialism (*anschauende Materialismus*) i.e. the Materialism which does not comprehend reality (*Sinnlichkeit*) as practical activity, is the contemplative

attitude of separate individuals within "bourgeois society." ' (Marx: *Thesen über Feuerbach* No. 9.)

[21] 'I'm frightened, really. I feel the devil in the air, and he'll try to get us. Or not the devil, Mammon; which I think, after all, is only the mass-will of people, wanting money and hating life. Anyhow I feel great grasping white hands in the air, wanting to get hold of the throat of anybody who tries to live, to live beyond money, and squeeze the life out. There's a bad time coming. There's a bad time coming, boys, there's a bad time coming! If things go on as they are, there's nothing big in the future but death and destruction, for these industrial masses.'

D. H. Lawrence: *Lady Chatterley's Lover*, p. 363 (Mellor's final letter to Connie).

[22] This, as far as I can see, is what the programme of the New Party (since Mr. John Strachey and his colleagues left it) really amounts to – fighting Communism, in the name of 'efficient' Capitalism. It is an utterly *empty* policy, without an atom of real conviction behind it. And, above all, it is an utterly ignorant policy. The choice before the New Party, intellectually, morally, politically, is either to support English Communism or to be ineffective and ridiculous. I can only imagine that, at the moment of the secession of Mr. Strachey and the clear-thinking members, Sir Oswald Mosley was bemused by the spectacular success of Hitler and the Nazis in Germany. This idea that England, the most *political* nation in the world, should or could imitate the processes of a *non-political* nation like Germany is a naivety of the same kind as

the imitation of Russian Communism in England. And of course it is far inferior, intellectually and morally, even to imitative Communism, which has a doctrine and a discipline but no objectivity.

[23] Inevitably, for the bloodiness of a revolution is directly proportionate to the inelasticity of the political system with which it breaks. Our parliamentary Revolution, which lost only Charles his head, was thundered at by Bossuet; but the system which Bossuet upheld foundered in blood and terror 150 years later. The same system endured 130 years longer in Russia. It foundered in still more blood and terror. The Russian Revolution *ought* to have been a bourgeois revolution, ideally speaking: that it wasn't was due, really, to the utter political and social backwardness of Russia. There *were* no bourgeois in Russia. If there had been, Lenin would have had no chance. (He would really have been, in those circumstances, the bourgeois leader, of course.) That Russia had no bourgeois was not a happy accident, but a social and political *crime*, of which the consequence will be that Russia will be the most backward state in the Communistic world. It will have to learn the rudiments of civilization still. In other words, Russia had to have a proletarian revolution because it was incapable of a bourgeois revolution. Whatever naive Communists may believe, a nation cannot simply omit a necessary stage in human development without paying for it. It has to pass through the ethical equivalent of that economic stage. When Russia has succeeded in bringing herself to the technical level of the West a period of spiritual crisis will begin. This will, I surmise, be apparent in

the partial inability of Russia to fulfil the Marxian prophecy, and pass from 'the dictatorship of the proletariat' to true Communism. The 'dictatorship of the proletariat' will be tyrannical and stifling in Russia when England is well on the way to true Communism.

[24] 'There are certain bourgeois who want to redress social grievances – in order to safeguard bourgeois society.

'To this category belong *economists*, philanthropists, humanitarians, welfare workers, charity organizers, members of societies for prevention of cruelty to animals, temperance fanatics, hole-and-corner reformers of every imaginable mind.

'Bourgeois socialists want the conditions of life that characterize modern society without the struggles and dangers which are the inevitable outcome of those conditions. They want extant society, without its revolutionary and disintegrating elements. They want the bourgeoisie without the proletariat.' (*The Manifesto of the Communist Party.*)